NEW JERSEY

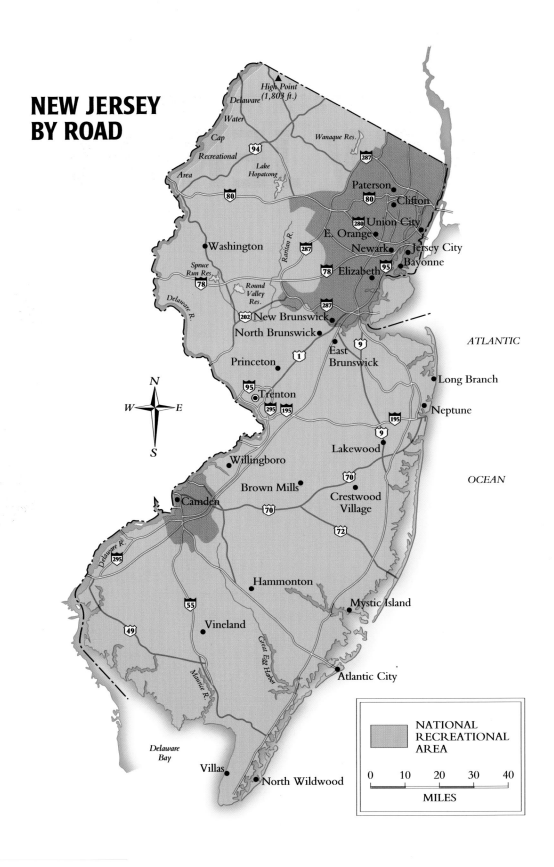

NEW JERSEY BY ROAD

High Point
(1,803 ft.)

Delaware

Water

Cap

Recreational

Area

Wanaque Res.

94

Lake Hopatcong

80

287

Paterson

80

Clifton

280

Union City

E. Orange

Newark

Jersey City

Bayonne

Washington

Raritan R.

287

Spruce Run Res.

78

78

Round Valley Res.

Elizabeth

95

Delaware R.

287

202

New Brunswick

North Brunswick

9

ATLANTIC

Princeton

1

East Brunswick

Long Branch

95

Trenton

Neptune

295

195

195

9

Lakewood

OCEAN

Willingboro

70

Brown Mills

Crestwood Village

Camden

70

72

Delaware R.

295

Hammonton

Mystic Island

55

Vineland

49

Great Egg Harbor

Atlantic City

Maurice R.

Delaware Bay

Villas

North Wildwood

N

W — E

S

NATIONAL
RECREATIONAL
AREA

0   10   20   30   40

MILES

CELEBRATE THE STATES
NEW JERSEY

Wendy Moragne

BENCHMARK BOOKS

MARSHALL CAVENDISH
NEW YORK

*To my parents, Rita and Henry Matz, who so lovingly provided a
wonderful and memorable childhood in New Jersey*

Benchmark Books
Marshall Cavendish Corporation
99 White Plains Road
Tarrytown, New York 10591-9001

Copyright © 2000 by Marshall Cavendish Corporation

Library of Congress Cataloging-in-Publication Data
Moragne, Wendy.
New Jersey / Wendy Moragne.
p.   cm.—(Celebrate the states)
Includes bibliographical references and index.
Summary: Discusses the geographic features, history, government, people, and attractions
of the state known as the Garden State.
ISBN 0-7614-0673-5 (lib. bdg.)
1. New Jersey—Juvenile literature. [1. New Jersey.] I. Title. II. Series.
F134.3.M67   2000   974.9—dc21   98-43948   CIP   AC

Maps and graphics supplied by Oxford Cartographers, Oxford, England

Photo Research by Candlepants Incorporated

Cover photo: Barrow

The photographs in this book are used by permission and through the courtesy of: *Kelly/Mooney*: 6-7, 13, 25, 61, 63, 68-69, 71, 80, 81, 83, 101, 103, 107, 109, 111, 112, 113, 114, 126, 139, back cover. *The Image Bank* : Joe Devenney, 10-11. *Photo Researchers Inc.*: E.R. Degginger, 15, 18(left); Robert T. Zappalorti, 22; Jeff Greenberg, 27; Chromosohm/Joe Sohm, 52-53; Andy Levin, 63; Stephen J. Krasemann, 64; Alan & Linda Detrick, 73; C. Vergara, 74; Larry Mulvehill, 98-99; Robert Bornemann, 116; Jeff Lepore,18(right), 119(right), 122; Lincoln Nutting/Audubon Society, 119 (left). Fred Maroon, 124. *Carol Kitman* : 17, 57, 76, 78. *Barrow* : 21, 24, 66-67. *Collection of Montclair Art Museum*: 28-29. *The Historical Society of Pennsylvania, 1834.1, by Gustavus Hesselius*: 31. *Archive Photos*: 32, 130, 136; Reuters/HO, 87(left); Consolidated News, 134; Gordon Grant, 135. *Burlington County Historical Society*: 35. *Corbis*: The Bettmann Collection, 40, 92,94, 127, 131, 132; UPI, 49,51, 89, 90, 91, 95, 128, 133; Bettmann-Reuters, 56; © Pacha, 87(right); © John Roca, 88. *Jane Voorhees Zimmerli Art Museum Rutgers, The State University of New Jersey*: 43. *Photofest*: 45. *Morris County Historical Society* : 46. *© Jeff Greenberg*: 58, 84-85.

Printed in Italy

1   3   5   6   4   2

CONTENTS

NEW JERSEY IS . . . .

New Jersey is a land of contrasts.

"Diversity . . . that's the spirit of New Jersey."
—historian John T. Cunningham

From its congested gray cities to its sprawling green farmland . . .

"I was born in this town, this old brick city of sidewalks and gray steel winter shadows."
—poet Amiri Baraka describing Newark

"The Countrey is full of great and tall Oakes."
—explorer Robert Juet

. . . from its ski slopes to its sandy beaches . . .

"New Jersey is a playground for all seasons."
—Governor Christine Todd Whitman

. . . from its bustling turnpike to its serene Pinelands . . .

"I thought New Jersey was just factories and smog. I was shocked to find beautiful flowering plants and trees like I've never seen before."
—visitor Joan Pifher

. . . New Jersey beckons for people to come and work, to come and play.

"New Jersey has been rated one of the top ten states in which to raise a child."   —Governor Christine Todd Whitman

---

New Jersey is a gem. Rich in beauty, rich in history, and rich in heritage, the Garden State has proven itself special through the years. The Native Americans who first inhabited the area knew the land was precious and fruitful, and they were able to keep it their own for thousands of years. But from the time Henry Hudson and his crew sailed along New Jersey's breathtaking coast in 1609, the land was destined to be shared.

About eight million people from around the world have chosen to make New Jersey their home. They have brought with them their cultures, their foods, and their dreams. They have shaped the way of life in New Jersey just as they have shaped the soil, and they have made New Jersey the great state it is today.

1 HILLS, VALLEYS, AND BEACHES

New Jersey is one of the smallest states, ranking forty-sixth in size. New York is its neighbor to the north and northeast, while Delaware is to the south and southwest. To the west lies Pennsylvania, and to the east lies the Atlantic Ocean.

Water forms natural boundaries on three sides of New Jersey. The Hudson River and the Atlantic Ocean form its eastern border, while the Delaware River forms its western border. The Delaware River spills into the Delaware Bay, which forms the state's southern border. New Jersey's only land border is the forty-eight miles it shares with New York in the north.

THE RUGGED NORTHWEST

Although small (you could drive the length of New Jersey in about three hours and the width of it in about one hour), New Jersey offers awesome topographic variety.

The Appalachian Ridge and Valley Region lies in the northwestern corner of the state. Majestic red oaks, the state tree, stand beside maples, birches, and elms. Flowering azaleas, rhododendrons, and purple violets, the state flower, provide color amid the greenery. This mountainous region includes the Kittatinny Mountains, where the Dutch mined copper in the mid-1600s.

The Delaware River, home to shad and trout, slices through the

The stunning beauty of the Delaware Water Gap awes visitors from near and far. Some enjoy rafting or boating down the river.

Kittatinny Mountains and forms the Delaware Water Gap, one of the most scenic areas in the eastern United States. The gap is a deep gorge that was formed millions of years ago by the Delaware River cutting through the rock. Its steep walls rise more than 1,200 feet on each side. Some people enjoy hot-air ballooning and plane gliding over this spectacular site.

At the base of the Kittatinny Mountains is the Appalachian Valley,

LAND AND WATER

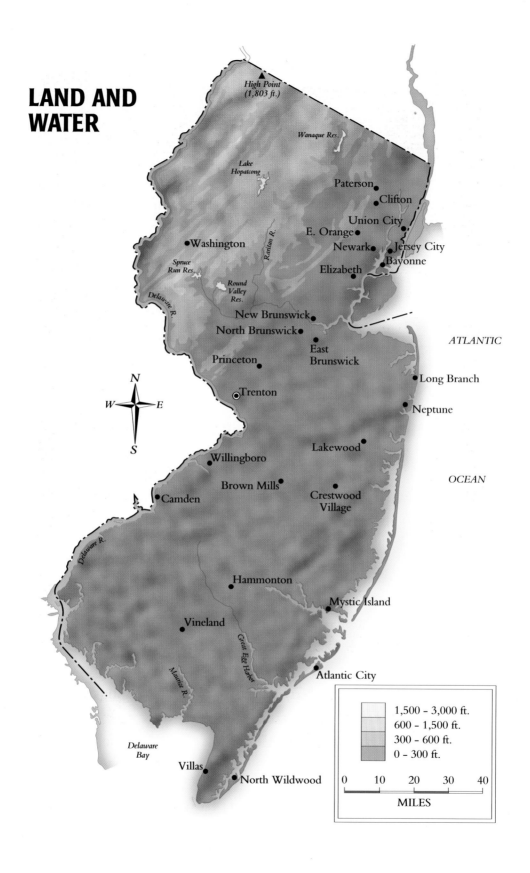

High Point
(1,803 ft.)

Wanaque Res.

Lake
Hopatcong

Paterson
Clifton
Union City
E. Orange
Washington
Newark
Jersey City
Raritan R.
Elizabeth
Bayonne

Spruce
Run Res.

Round
Valley
Res.

Delaware R.

New Brunswick
North Brunswick

ATLANTIC

Princeton
East
Brunswick

Trenton

Long Branch

Neptune

Lakewood

Willingboro

OCEAN

Brown Mills
Crestwood
Village

Camden

Delaware R.

Hammonton

Mystic Island

Vineland

Great Egg Harbor

Maurice R.

Atlantic City

Delaware
Bay

Villas

North Wildwood

| 1,500 – 3,000 ft. |
| 600 – 1,500 ft. |
| 300 – 600 ft. |
| 0 – 300 ft. |

0   10   20   30   40

MILES

THE FRANKLIN MINERALS

Franklin, New Jersey, is home to some very unusual rocks. Millions of years ago, large pockets of zinc deep within the earth there were altered in such a way that more than three hundred new minerals were formed. Amazingly, about thirty of these minerals have been found nowhere else on Earth. Even more intriguing is that many of the Franklin minerals are fluorescent—they glow yellow, green, pink, lavender, and rose when placed under ultraviolet light.

The Franklin Mineral Museum showcases these fantastic minerals and even gives rock hounds a chance to search for minerals outside.

where the soil is rich and dairy cattle graze on lush grass. A Dutch traveler in the 1600s called this area "the handsomest and pleasantest country that man can behold."

The Highlands Region is southeast of the Appalachian Ridge and Valley Region. Here, lakes lie nestled among flat-topped ridges of hard rock. The lakes were carved into the rocks thousands of years ago by a huge glacier. Hopatcong is the largest lake in New Jersey. Other large lakes in the Highlands are Budd, Green Pond, Lake Mohawk, and Upper Greenwood.

THE PIEDMONT

Southeast of the Highlands is the Piedmont, an area of gently rolling hills. Major rivers such as the Hudson, Hackensack, Raritan, and Passaic flow through the Piedmont. Slicing between two massive rocks in Paterson are the Great Falls of the Passaic, a mighty gush of water spilling seventy feet down. Two Dutchmen who saw the falls in the 1600s described them as "a sight to be seen in order to observe the power and wonder of God." These rivers helped the large industrial cities of Paterson, Newark, Elizabeth, and Jersey City flourish. The giant wheels that powered gristmills and textile mills were turned by water.

Looming high above the Hudson River near Fort Lee is the Palisades, a five-hundred-foot-tall, thirteen-mile-long cliff. In the early 1900s, silent movies were made in Fort Lee. One popular film series always showed the star in danger, often perched high on a cliff. The cliff was the Palisades, and scenes that left the audience in suspense became known as cliff-hangers.

South of the Palisades are two great wetlands. Lying along the Hackensack River, the Meadowlands is a stretch of damp land that was left after a giant lake evaporated thousands of years ago. The area is rich in wildlife and vegetation, which manage to exist side by side with highways, office buildings, apartments, and a huge sports-entertainment complex named the Meadowlands. The Great Swamp, near Morristown, is also a former lake. Although at one time people suggested paving over this marshy, wooded area to make an airport, citizens groups convinced the government to protect the region, and the Great Swamp National Wildlife Refuge was created.

The power of the Great Falls of the Passaic enabled Paterson to become the first industrial city in the nation.

THE ATLANTIC COASTAL PLAIN

About three-fifths of New Jersey is a gently rolling lowland called the Atlantic Coastal Plain. In the southwest, the Atlantic Coastal Plain contains fertile soil, perfect for growing a variety of fruits and vegetables. This rich area gave New Jersey its official nickname, the Garden State. In this region, stately oak, maple, and pine trees create a safe haven for chipmunks, squirrels, and rabbits. Cardinals, blue jays, robins, and eastern goldfinches, the state bird, build nests in the crooks of the branches.

The eastern part of the coastal plain is made up of pine forests, saltwater marshland, and sandy, gravelly soil. Deer, skunks, opossums, and raccoons make the woodland their home, while wild ducks and geese prefer the marshland. At the far eastern edge of the Atlantic Coastal Plain lie New Jersey's 127 miles of white sandy beaches and dunes. The salty coastal waters abound with flounder, bluefish, crabs, oysters, and clams. Sandpipers dance at the water's edge, while seagulls glide overhead.

The most intriguing feature of the Atlantic Coastal Plain is the Pinelands, also called the Pine Barrens. The Pinelands is a vast area of forests, bogs, marshes, and swamps crisscrossed by streams and dotted with ponds. The water is tea colored because of the organic material from cedar trees and iron seeping out of the sandy soil.

More than eight hundred plant species thrive in the Pinelands' sandy soil, providing food and shelter for more than three hundred species of mammals, birds, reptiles, and amphibians. Many of these plants and animals are unusual. They rely on the Pinelands' fragile environment for their existence. The rare curly-grass fern is a

Chipmunks and other small animals thrive in New Jersey's lush vegetation.

Deer are plentiful throughout the state, as they were when the Indians relied on deerskin and meat for clothing and food.

THE TRASH MUSEUM

Imagine falling into a landfill and being surrounded by nothing but used tires, old chicken wire, cardboard boxes, and aluminum cans. Visitors get a chance to experience something strangely similar when they visit the Trash Museum at the Meadowlands Environment Center and Museum in Lyndhurst. The Trash Museum conveys a clear and unforgettable message—recycle!

The center is built on an area of the Meadowlands where the Lenni Lenape once dug clams and oysters. By the 1930s, people had turned the region into a dumping ground. In time, the garbage contaminated the soil and choked out the wildlife and vegetation that once thrived there. The dangerous waste also seeped into nearby water, harming the shellfish that had once sustained the Lenni Lenape.

The turning point came in 1969, when the Hackensack Meadowlands Development Commission was formed. They encouraged New Jerseyans to recycle their waste so that not so much would have to be dumped in landfills. Household dumping was eventually stopped in the Meadowlands. Remarkably, wildlife and vegetation have returned to the area. Even the water is clean again. The Meadowlands is proof that the most spoiled land can be saved and that recycling can help.

tiny plant that grows just above the waterline on the small mounds of earth where cedar trees grow in bogs. The curly-grass fern requires this exact environment for its survival.

The million-acre region has towns and farms and more than 700,000 residents, but much of the area is protected by the government. Because of the unusual plants and animals that live there,

Canoeing along the miles of streams is one of the best ways to experience the serenity and beauty of the Pinelands.

THE PINE BARRENS TREE FROG

The Pine Barrens tree frog is a tiny creature, just over 1.5 inches long. Its distinct call is a series of honks that sound like "quonk, quonk, quonk." It is emerald green, with a white and purple border that runs along its sides from head to toe. And the underside of its hind legs is yellowish orange.

The Pine Barrens tree frog loves the swampy soil and acidic water of the Pinelands and needs this environment for its survival. Although this species of tree frog also exists in some southern states, it does not live anywhere in New Jersey except in the Pinelands. If the amount of acid in the water or the level of the water in the Pinelands were to change, the Pine Barrens tree frog would not be able to survive there. As one of New Jersey's endangered species, its habitat is carefully protected. By limiting the development that can take place in the Pinelands, the state is trying to ensure that the Pine Barrens tree frog and other creatures will have an unspoiled region where they can live.

the Pinelands was designated America's first National Reserve in 1978 and an International Biosphere Reserve in 1983. Several state parks and forests, such as Double Trouble and Wharton, invite visitors to hike or canoe through the quiet, mystical Pinelands. Visitors can even swim in the strange, tea-colored water!

CHANGING SEASONS

"I love the change of seasons," says Victoria Browning of Cherry Hill. "I enjoy the lovely spring flowers, especially the tulips, and the mix of colors of the autumn leaves. I always look forward to going to the shore in the summer, and I really don't mind the winter. Everything is so quiet and peaceful during a snowfall."

Many New Jerseyans believe they have the best of everything when it comes to weather. Although summers tend to be humid, the shore offers relief. The cool breezes and refreshing ocean waves provide comfort. Thundershowers and rain keep the inland areas green throughout the summer, especially in the northern part of the state. Then, beginning in late September, the lush green gives way to brilliant autumn colors as the leaves turn shades of red, orange, and yellow. The air becomes crisp during the fall, hinting at the chilly winter months ahead.

The average January temperature in New Jersey is 31 degrees Fahrenheit. The average July temperature is 75 degrees Fahrenheit. The northern part of the state receives more snowfall than the southern part.

Over the years, New Jersey has fallen victim to hurricanes, nor'easters, blizzards, ice storms, and even an occasional tornado.

During the crisp autumn months, New Jersey's landscape is magically transformed from a blanket of green to a mosaic of red, orange, and yellow.

The relentless wind and rain of hurricanes and nor'easters flatten trees and damage buildings as they pound sometimes for days. Along the coast, surging tides and waves wash away beaches, boardwalks, and houses. Blizzards and ice storms snap electrical

Sandy beaches and rolling waves along the coast delight thousands of vacationers during the muggy months of summer.

wires and cripple traffic. "Bad storms don't come through very often, but when they do, they're real beauties," says Hank Susen, a senior citizen who has lived in New Jersey all his life.

PROTECTING THE ENVIRONMENT

New Jersey is the nation's most densely populated state, and pollutants from cars, development, and industry threaten its environment. The state strives to control air pollution, while also putting great effort into cleaning up and protecting its waters. Any rainwater that runs onto roads picks up the oil and gasoline that has accumulated there from cars and trucks. The water then carries these pollutants into nearby waterways. Chemicals and fertilizer used on lawns also run off into waterways during rains. New Jerseyans have been asked to help in simple ways, such as planting grass and trees and avoiding the use of lawn chemicals and fertilizers. The grass and trees help rainwater soak into the ground so that fewer pollutants wash into waterways.

New Jersey's heavy boat traffic also threatens the waters. The state is working with marine associations to reduce the amount of sewage that is released into the water by boats. Many uncaring people have dumped their boats' waste tanks into the ocean, bays, and rivers. To encourage people not to do this, stations have been set up along the waterways where boaters can pump out their waste tanks.

New Jersey's efforts have already paid off. The number of ocean fish, such as striped bass, Atlantic mackerel, and Atlantic herring, has increased. Even dolphins abound in the offshore waters now.

And New Jersey's clammers have something to rejoice about, too. "For the first time in twenty-five years, we opened more than six hundred acres for seasonal unrestricted clamming in the Navesink River," says Governor Christine Todd Whitman. Still, New Jersey will have to remain vigilant to ensure that the state's waters are clean and safe for people and wildlife alike.

Clamming is an important industry in New Jersey. Cleaner waters mean bigger harvests.

2 MIGHTY NEW JERSEY

Great Notch, New Jersey, by Lawrence C. Earle

For thousands of years before the first Europeans arrived in what would become New Jersey, the land was inhabited by Indians. When the white explorers and settlers arrived, the people they encountered called themselves the Lenni Lenape, a name that means "original people."

THE LENNI LENAPE

The Lenni Lenape relied on hunting for their survival. The deer, foxes, squirrels, minks, raccoons, and even bears that lived in the forests provided them with nutritious meat and warm furs. The Lenni Lenape also hunted wild geese and turkeys. The leftover feathers adorned men's heads. Deerskins served as clothing for both men and women. The Lenni Lenape supplemented their diet by planting vegetables. Beans, squash, and corn grew well in the rich soil. The Lenni Lenape also enjoyed the abundant blueberries, strawberries, and cranberries that grew wild on the land.

Each spring, the Lenni Lenape left the forested interior and journeyed by foot to the seashore, where they spent several months. Footstep upon footstep, they packed the earth beneath their feet and created permanent paths through the woods and over land. These trails were later used as roads by white settlers. Along the coast, the Lenni Lenape took advantage of the plentiful fish and

Most Lenni Lenape men wore their hair long and greased it with bear fat.

shellfish. Some of the seafood was eaten during the summer, and some was smoke-dried and carried back to the villages for winter use.

The Indians lived in round wigwams or rectangular longhouses. These structures were constructed from young trees, called saplings, set in the ground with other saplings tied to them. This framework was then covered with bark, offering shelter and shade. Traveling in canoes crafted from logs, the Lenni Lenape used rivers and streams as their highways. They shaped their canoes by charring the logs and then scooping out the charred wood.

THE EXPLORERS

When Giovanni de Verrazano, an Italian, crossed the ocean from France in 1524, he became the first European to explore what would become New Jersey. His visit was short and had little impact on the land or the Indians who lived there. Nearly one hundred years would pass before the Lenni Lenape would face change.

In 1609, Henry Hudson, an Englishman employed by the Dutch, sailed across the Atlantic. His mission was to find a water passage that would cut through North America and lead to Asia, where gold, jewels, and other riches awaited. But Hudson never found the

When Henry Hudson reached the New Jersey coast in 1609 in his ship Half Moon, *crewmen Robert Juet noted in his journal, "This day the people of the Countrey came aboard to us, seeming very glad of our comming."*

passage. Instead, he went ashore in what would become New Jersey and met and traded with the Lenni Lenape. Hudson's visit opened the door for traders and settlers to come to the new land.

THE SETTLERS

The Dutch and Swedish settlers who arrived in the 1630s were the first white people to inhabit New Jersey. For the first time, the Lenni Lenape had to share their land. Early on, the relationship between the Indians and the Europeans was friendly. The welcoming ways of the Lenni Lenape enabled the settlers to establish themselves. The Indians taught the settlers about hunting, fishing, trapping, and cultivating plants. They gave the Europeans land in exchange for clothing, guns, knives, and trinkets, such as glass beads. They also traded animal furs with the whites. The furs were taken to Europe, where they were sold to coat and hat manufacturers.

The fur trade was so profitable that conflict arose between the Dutch and Swedes. By 1655, the Dutch had forced all but a few Swedes off the land, and in 1660, they set up New Jersey's first permanent European village, which they named Bergen. Over time, Bergen grew and prospered and became what we know today as Jersey City. Meanwhile, tension had mounted between the Dutch and the Lenni Lenape. They quarreled over land, trade, and lifestyle, resulting in bloodshed on both sides.

ENGLAND RULES

In 1664, England took control of the land that had been settled by the Dutch. Two Englishmen, Lord John Berkeley and Sir George

Carteret, were given a portion of the land. Carteret had served as governor of Jersey, an island in the English Channel, so the land was named New Jersey in his honor.

Berkeley and Carteret were interested in the land as a business enterprise. They hoped that rental fees and trade would bring them money. But this would only be possible if settlers agreed to live there. To encourage people to make this wilderness their home, Berkeley and Carteret promised them that the rent on the land would be low and that they would have religious and political freedom. Their offer was so appealing that many settlers journeyed from colonies farther north to make New Jersey their home.

Ten years later, in 1674, Berkeley sold his share of New Jersey to Edward Byllynge and John Fenwick, who were members of a religious sect called the Quakers. In 1676, the colony was divided into two sections, West Jersey and East Jersey. The Quakers settled in West Jersey, making it the first Quaker colony in America. Six years later William Penn, also a Quaker, and his associates bought East Jersey. People began to journey across the Atlantic from England, Scotland, and Ireland to take advantage of what New Jersey had to offer.

A SETTLER'S LIFE

Farming was the settlers' most important activity. To feed their families, they grew grains, fruits, and vegetables and raised livestock. Some settlers were also involved in businesses. Tanneries turned cowhides into leather products, sawmills turned trees into lumber, and gristmills turned wheat into flour.

The Quakers were instrumental in settling New Jersey in the late 1600s. The early settlers gathered for worship in a meetinghouse, a tradition carried on by Quakers today.

As the 1600s came to a close, arguments arose over who actually owned the land. The settlers resented paying rent to live on the land. The tension finally led to rioting, and by 1702, those who supposedly owned East and West Jersey gave up ownership. England then united the two colonies.

During the 1700s, farming expanded as the colonists began selling their crops in the nearby cities of New York and Philadelphia. Iron mining became profitable as well. Iron ore was plentiful in the hills of northern New Jersey. In southern New Jersey, bog iron, a low-grade form of iron that collects along riverbanks, was common. Throughout the colony, vast forests supplied the charcoal that fueled iron furnaces. Many men made their living by chopping down trees. The abundance of trees also prompted settlers to set up sawmills, where the wood was cut into lumber and shipped to nearby cities or overseas.

Glass products were shipped from New Jersey as well. Caspar Wistar opened a glassmaking factory in Salem in 1739. The Wistarberg Works turned out bottles, jars, and windowpanes for the colonies.

Fishing and whaling were also profitable industries. Boats with five or six crewmen left from Long Beach Island and Cape May to harpoon whales. Whale carcasses were towed onto the beach, where they were immediately cut up. The flesh was cooked in huge iron kettles, and the oil rendered from the flesh was sold throughout the colonies.

GROWTH MEANS CHANGE

As New Jersey grew, the Lenni Lenape faced dramatic change. Diseases brought from Europe, such as measles and smallpox, had killed many of them. Those who lived found themselves at odds with the settlers over how the land should be used. Because the Lenni Lenape relied on hunting for their survival, preserving the forests meant everything to them. But the colonists depended on farming and on the iron, lumber, and glass industries. They wanted to clear the forests to fuel their furnaces and create farmland.

Most Lenni Lenape left New Jersey for New York and Pennsylvania in search of a better life. In 1758, the few hundred Lenni Lenape who had stayed in New Jersey were offered a 3,044-acre tract of land in Burlington County where they could live undisturbed. The Lenni Lenape lived on this reservation, called Brotherton, until 1802, when they left New Jersey to join the others who had gone before them.

THE REVOLUTIONARY WAR

During the 1760s, unrest began to simmer in the colonies because of a series of laws passed by Britain. Most either restricted colonial trade or set high taxes on items such as tea, a favorite of the colonists.

By 1774, tension was so high that a group of angry New Jerseyans dressed as Indians and burned a shipload of British tea in Greenwich. This event became known as the Greenwich Tea Burning and was similar to the Boston Tea Party, which had taken place a year earlier in Massachusetts.

Although some colonists felt that they should stay loyal to Britain in spite of the strict laws, many believed that becoming independent of Britain was the only way to go. They put their intentions in writing when they signed the Declaration of Independence in July 1776.

General George Washington led the Continental army through the Revolutionary War. Much of the ammunition his troops used was made in New Jersey's ironworks, and the food for his soldiers came from New Jersey's farms.

Washington and his troops met with disappointment early in the war, but then Washington came up with a plan. He knew that the Hessians—Germans fighting for England—would celebrate

THE BATTLE OF TRENTON

Late Christmas night, 1776, George Washington's ragged army rowed across the icy Delaware River and fell upon the 1,200-man Hessian force in Trenton, which was sleeping off its Christmas celebration. It was a much-needed victory, coming after a long series of military setbacks for Washington and the Continental army.

Our object was the Hessian band,
That dared invade fair freedom's land,
      And quarter in that place.
Great Washington he led us on,
Whose streaming flag in storm or sun
      Had never known disgrace.

In silent march we passed the night,
Each soldier panting for the fight,
      Though quite benumbed with frost.
Greene, on the left, at six began.
The right was led by Sullivan,
      Who ne'er a moment lost.

Their pickets stormed, the alarm was spread,
That rebels risen from the dead
      Were marching into town.
Some scampered here, some scampered there,
And some for action did prepare;
      But soon their arms lay down.

Twelve hundred servile miscreants,
With all their colors, guns and tents,
      Were trophies of the day.
The frolic o'er, the bright canteen
In center, front and rear was seen,
      Driving fatigue away.

Now, brothers of the patriot bands,
Let's sing deliverance from the hands
      Of arbitrary sway.
And as our life is but a span,
Let's touch the tankard while we can,
      In memory of that day.

George Washington led his weary troops across the Delaware River on Christmas night in 1776. Half-starved and dressed in tattered clothing, the brave men navigated the ice-choked river on their way to the Battle of Trenton.

Christmas in the Barracks, a large building in Trenton. Figuring that the Hessians would eventually fall into a deep sleep after the night's festivities, Washington planned a surprise attack. Late on Christmas night, 1776, the general and 2,400 men crossed the icy Delaware River in a snowstorm and walked eight miles to the Barracks. On the morning of December 26, Washington's army bombarded the unsuspecting Hessians and succeeded in taking nearly one thousand of them prisoner. The spot in Titusville where

Washington and his men came ashore is now called Washington Crossing State Park. Every Christmas, the crossing of the Delaware is reenacted there.

The Battle of Monmouth was fought on a scorching summer day, June 28, 1778. Legend has it that Molly Pitcher, the wife of a soldier, dipped water from a nearby well to soothe the men's parched mouths. During the Revolutionary War, soldiers' wives were allowed to travel with their husbands, so it was not unusual for Molly to be on the battlefield. What was unusual, however, was that later in the battle, Molly manned one of the cannons! Today, at the Monmouth Battlefield State Park near Freehold, visitors can see the Molly Pitcher Well.

Washington and his troops finally achieved victory in 1783. On December 18, 1787, New Jersey signed the U.S. Constitution and became the third state. Trenton became the state capital in 1790 and remains so today.

BECOMING AN INDUSTRIAL LEADER

In 1791, Alexander Hamilton, the U.S. treasury secretary, chose the land around the Great Falls of the Passaic as the site for a factory town. He planned for the water of the falls to supply power to run factories, which would manufacture cotton cloth. His plan worked, and Paterson became the first industrialized city in America.

In 1825, John Stevens built America's first steam locomotive in Hoboken. Two years later Thomas Rogers began building steam locomotives in Paterson, which became the hub of locomotive production. By the end of the century, thousands of steam locomotives had been manufactured there. In 1840, silk manufacturing also took hold, and Paterson became known as Silk City.

Meanwhile, other New Jersey cities were buzzing with activity. Trenton was manufacturing iron, textiles, and pottery. Newark was turning out leather goods and jewelry. Jersey City was making soap, bricks, and steel. And in the southern part of the state, glassworks were busy.

New Jersey's industry was able to prosper because of improvements in transportation. Canals and railroads built in the 1830s connected New Jersey's cities to New York and Philadelphia. People came from Ireland and Germany to build the canals and railroads and work in the flourishing factories.

THE CIVIL WAR

From the time Europeans first settled the East Coast, Africans had been brought to America to work as slaves. Many Northerners, including the Quakers, were against slavery and helped slaves gain freedom. In 1804, New Jersey passed a law to gradually free its slaves. But in the Southern states, slavery continued.

When Abraham Lincoln, who opposed slavery, was elected president of the United States in 1860, some Southerners saw their way of life slipping away. They decided to break away from the United States and form the Confederate States of America. But Northerners did not want the Southern states to separate from the Union. The result was the Civil War. Although no battles were fought on its soil, New Jersey sent 88,000 men into the Union army.

The North's prosperity eventually made the difference in who

The network of railroad tracks and bridges built during the first half of the 1800s boosted industry in towns along its path. German and Irish immigrants did much of the backbreaking construction.

won the war. The thriving factories and farms of New Jersey and other Northern states supplied the Union army. The Confederate army did not have the same backing. In the end, the lack of food and such supplies as shoes doomed the Confederate army, and they surrendered in 1865. The war was finally over, and so was slavery.

FLOURISHING INDUSTRIES

New Jersey prospered after the war. In 1869 in Vineland, a dentist named Thomas Bramwell Welch found a way to make grape juice rather than wine out of local grapes. This was the beginning of the Welch's Grape Juice Company. The year proved just as prosperous for Joseph Campbell in Camden. Taking advantage of New Jersey's plentiful peas and tomatoes, he opened a canning plant, marking the birth of the Campbell Soup Company.

In the 1870s, life-changing innovations were being developed in Menlo Park, where Thomas Edison invented the phonograph and perfected the electric light. In Paterson, John Philip Holland built a fourteen-foot submarine that he took to the bottom of the Passaic River in 1878. His efforts led to the development of today's submarines.

During the final decades of the nineteenth century, the Johnson & Johnson medical supply company established itself in New Brunswick with the manufacture of gauze and adhesive tape. Eldridge R. Johnson began building talking machines, which played flat disks, or records, instead of the cylinders Edison's phonograph had used. His Victor Talking Machine Company in Camden soon became the world's largest producer of phonograph records. The era's greatest breakthrough was the development of motion pictures in 1889 by Thomas Edison, who had moved his laboratory to West Orange. By the early 1900s, motion pictures had become so popular that a busy filmmaking industry cropped up in Fort Lee.

As the nineteenth century folded into the twentieth, New Jersey's industries kept on rolling. In the cities, the manufacture of oil, steel, rubber, chemicals, electrical goods, and apparel bolstered the economy. In rural areas, canneries and glass factories continued to add strength. Dairy and poultry businesses also took hold, with

FORT LEE, THE MOVIE CAPITAL

Believe it or not, Fort Lee, New Jersey, was once the movie capital of America, and Hollywood, California, was just an ordinary town. Thanks to the moving pictures developed by Thomas Edison, the filmmaking industry took off in Fort Lee in the early 1900s.

New Jersey's cities, beaches, mountains, and farms were the backdrops for movie after movie. A section of Fort Lee looked exactly like an Old West town, so even filming Westerns was a cinch. Big-name stars such as Mary Pickford, Douglas Fairbanks, Lillian Gish, and Lionel and Ethel Barrymore walked Fort Lee's streets.

But Fort Lee's heyday was not to last. When a top filmmaker journeyed to California and made a film in Hollywood, a shadow was cast over Fort Lee. The sunny, mild weather of California proved irresistible, and the other filmmakers also headed west. By 1925, New Jersey's film industry was no more.

In the late nineteenth and early twentieth centuries, Italian immigrants such as these stonecutters poured into New Jersey to work in its bustling cities.

residents of nearby cities welcoming shipments of farm-fresh milk, eggs, and poultry.

With the growth of New Jersey's farm production and industries came the need for more workers. Between the late 1800s and early 1900s, hundreds of thousands of people came from Germany, Italy, Ireland, Poland, and Russia to work in New Jersey. So many immigrants flooded into New Jersey that by 1910, more than half of the state's residents had been born outside the United States or had parents who had been born outside the United States.

WARS AND DEPRESSION

The United States entered World War I in 1917. During the war, New Jersey's huge shipyards turned out battleships, while its factories manufactured ammunition, chemicals, and fabric for uniforms and blankets.

A decade after the war ended, the United States found itself in the Great Depression. People all over the country lost their jobs, and banks failed. Even New Jersey was hit hard. Many of its factories closed, forcing some workers to turn to long breadlines for food. People had to do without many everyday items. "I can remember

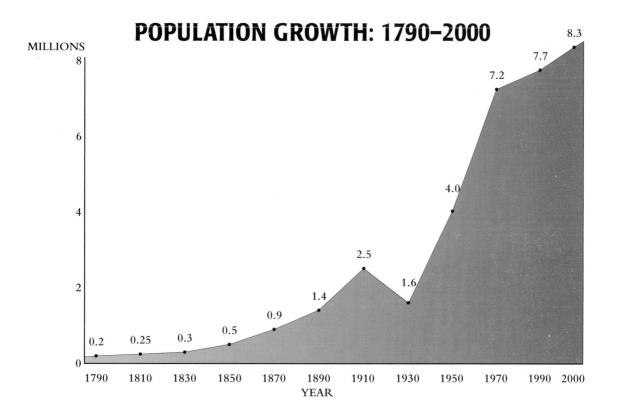

POPULATION GROWTH: 1790–2000

my mother cutting pieces of cardboard to put in the bottom of my shoes," says a senior citizen who grew up in Camden. "We had a pair of everyday shoes and a pair of dress shoes, and when the soles wore out, that was it. We had to make do with the cardboard. Otherwise, we just had socks on the bottoms of our feet."

The nation's economy picked up when the United States entered World War II in 1941. New Jersey again produced ammunition, chemicals, and battleships, as well as communications equipment. Paterson became the nation's leading airplane engine manufacturing center. New Jersey also supported the war effort with its people. More than 500,000 New Jersey residents served in the armed forces.

NEW JERSEY TODAY

After World War II, New Jersey's economy was strong. The chemicals, medicines, electronics, and foods the state produced were selling well. Its research firms were developing technology that would change the way people lived. The solar cell, laser, transistor, and satellite communications were all developed at Bell Laboratories in Murray Hill.

During this time, the state's densely populated cities began to spill into rural areas. Housing developments were built on farmland outside the cities, and many families who could afford to move were lured away from the overcrowded cities. Suburbs around Philadelphia and New York City were especially popular because residents could commute to jobs in these cities.

While New Jersey's suburbs blossomed, its cities wilted. As

Battleships built in New Jersey's shipyards sailed overseas to fight during World War I and World War II. In 1941, the U.S.S. Atlanta took to the water in a ceremonial launching in Kearny.

TEN LARGEST CITIES

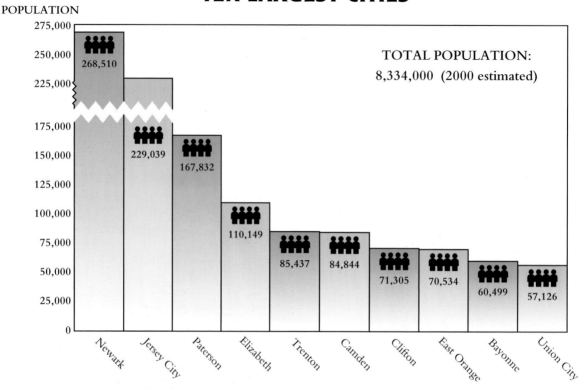

POPULATION

TOTAL POPULATION:
8,334,000 (2000 estimated)

- Newark 268,510
- Jersey City 229,039
- Paterson 167,832
- Elizabeth 110,149
- Trenton 85,437
- Camden 84,844
- Clifton 71,305
- East Orange 70,534
- Bayonne 60,499
- Union City 57,126

people and industries moved away, buildings were abandoned. In time, the cities' African-American residents who were left behind rebelled against the neglect of their neighborhoods. In July 1967, riots broke out in several cities around the state. The worst was in Newark, where twenty-six people were killed and more than one thousand were injured.

Not until the 1980s was an effort made to brighten New Jersey's cities. Urban renewal projects have brought businesses and improvements to the state's most run-down cities, but much work

Tension mounted in Newark in the summer of 1967 when the National Guard was called on to aid local police in controlling rioting.

remains to be done. As New Jersey moves into the twenty-first century, it will continue to draw on the strengths of its land and people, as it has for hundreds of years. "New Jersey may be small, but it's mighty," says a proud New Jerseyan. "There isn't a day that goes by that I don't feel lucky to live here."

3 RULES AND ROLES

The state capitol in Trenton

A state's constitution is its supreme law. It sets up the rules and principles of the state. New Jersey has had three constitutions over the years. Its third and present constitution was adopted in 1947.

INSIDE GOVERNMENT

New Jersey's laws are created and carried out by the executive, legislative, and judicial branches of government.

Executive. New Jersey is one of just two states (the other is Maine) in which the governor is the only executive official elected by the people. The governor appoints the attorney general, secretary of state, state treasurer, and the heads of major state departments. All of the governor's appointments must be approved by the state senate. The governor is also commander in chief of the state's militia and proposes the budget to the legislature.

The governor is elected to a four-year term and may only serve two terms in a row. In 1993, Christine Todd Whitman became the first woman to be elected governor of New Jersey. She was reelected in 1997.

Legislative. The legislature is made up of a forty-member senate and an eighty-member general assembly. Senators serve for four years. But if the term begins with the decade, it is only two years long. Members of the assembly serve for two years. A bill

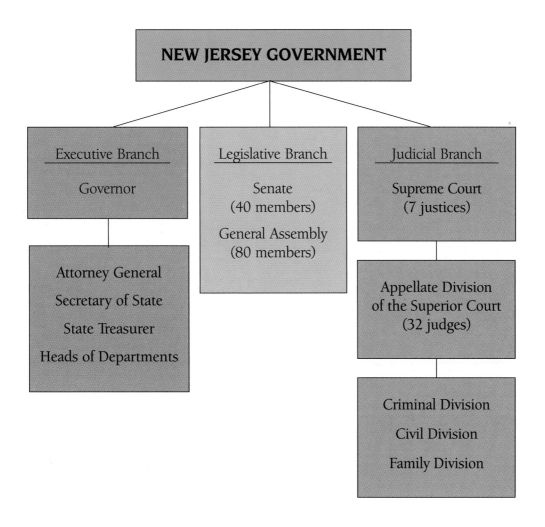

NEW JERSEY GOVERNMENT

Executive Branch

Governor

Attorney General

Secretary of State

State Treasurer

Heads of Departments

Legislative Branch

Senate
(40 members)

General Assembly
(80 members)

Judicial Branch

Supreme Court
(7 justices)

Appellate Division
of the Superior Court
(32 judges)

Criminal Division

Civil Division

Family Division

may be introduced in either the senate or the general assembly. Once a bill is passed, it goes to the governor, who either signs it into law, returns it to the legislature with suggestions for change, or vetoes (rejects) it. If two-thirds of both the senate and the assembly vote to override the governor's veto, the bill can still become law.

Judicial. New Jersey's highest court, the supreme court, is made up of one chief justice and six associate justices. The supreme court hears cases involving constitutional problems and capital punish-

In 1993, New Jerseyans elected Christine Todd Whitman their first female governor.

ment and has the power to overturn decisions made in lower courts. Its decisions are final.

The state's chief trial court, the superior court, hears criminal and civil cases and reviews decisions that have been made in lower courts.

Members of both the supreme and superior courts are appointed to seven-year terms by the governor, with the senate's approval. Judges who are reappointed once are then allowed to serve until they are seventy years old.

LAWS THAT HELP YOUNG PEOPLE

"In our schools, we strive to give our children the knowledge to succeed in the future," says Governor Christine Todd Whitman. New Jersey works hard to ensure that its students receive the best education possible. Students who are not proficient in English are entitled to receive a bilingual education. In a Spanish-speaking community, for example, teachers are able to speak both English and Spanish with their students. "When we came here from Cuba,

Education is important to New Jersey's lawmakers and residents alike. The state makes an effort to meet the needs of its diverse students.

Lots of New Jersey kids enjoy after-school activities such as swimming.

the teachers at my school talked to me in Spanish at first and then added English later," says Miguel Fuentes of Union City. "With the teachers using my language, it made me feel more comfortable. It made me feel like I could fit in, and it gave me a chance to do well in school. My grades were good right from the beginning. At home, my family kept on speaking Spanish—only Spanish."

In cases of divorce or when both parents are not living with the child, strict child support laws apply. If the parent who is supposed to pay child support fails to do so, the state can withhold money from that parent's paycheck. "My brother and I live with my mom,"

Natural Resources

Clams

Fish

Sand and Gravel

Stone

Agriculture

Corn

Cranberries

Greenhouse and Nursery products

Milk

Peaches

Tomatoes

Manufacturing

Food products

Pharmaceuticals

Printed materials

Wanaque Res.

Lake Hopatcong

MILK

MILK

Paterson

Clifton

Union City

E. Orange

Newark

Jersey City

Bayonne

Washington

Elizabeth

Rariton R.

Spruce Run Res.

Round Valley Res.

New Brunswick

North Brunswick

ATLANTIC

Princeton

East Brunswick

Delaware R.

Long Branch

Trenton

Neptune

MILK

Lakewood

Willingboro

OCEAN

Brown Mills

Crestwood Village

Camden

Delaware R.

Hammonton

Mystic Island

Vineland

Maurice R.

Great Egg Harbor

Atlantic City

Delaware Bay

Villas

North Wildwood

EARNING A LIVING

says a thirteen-year-old from New Brunswick. "Even though my mom works, my dad has to pay child support for us. I take art lessons after school and my brother plays on a soccer team, and the child support money helps pay for these things."

AN ECONOMIC TAPESTRY

New Jersey has many different types of businesses, which are woven together to create a strong and diverse economy. It draws its strength from three main factors. First, New Jersey has an excellent transportation system and large ports, so receiving raw materials and shipping finished goods is easy. Second, it has a large and well-trained group of workers. Third, New York City, Philadelphia, and other nearby cities provide a solid market for New Jersey's products.

Nearly four-fifths of New Jersey's economy is made up of service industries. Prudential, the largest insurance company in the

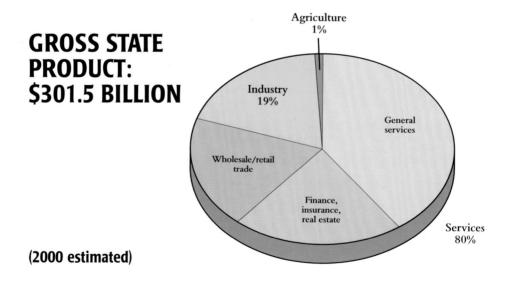

GROSS STATE PRODUCT: $301.5 BILLION

Agriculture 1%

Industry 19%

General services

Wholesale/retail trade

Finance, insurance, real estate

Services 80%

(2000 estimated)

Vacationers take a break from the Atlantic City boardwalk to participate in the sand-sculpting contest held every summer on the beach.

United States, is based in Newark. Bell Laboratories, located at Murray Hill, is one of the world's foremost private research complexes. Thousands of New Jerseyans work on life-changing inventions and developments there.

Tourism is a leading service industry. Vacationers flock to New Jersey's seashore, lakes, and parks during the summer. In the winter, ski slopes in the northern part of the state attract crowds. And Atlantic City lures tourists to its boardwalk, complete with games, amusement rides, and food. In 1976, voters agreed to allow gambling casinos to be built in Atlantic City. The first casino opened in 1978, and the casinos continue to attract huge numbers of visitors who bring money into the state.

Government services, such as military bases, are also important in New Jersey. McGuire Air Force Base, Fort Dix, and the Naval Air Warfare Center at Lakehurst are all in New Jersey. The U.S. Coast Guard operates a training center in Cape May.

Manufacturing is the second-largest part of New Jersey's economy. New Jersey is a leading producer of chemicals and medicines. Four pharmaceutical giants—Bristol-Myers Squibb, Johnson & Johnson, Merck, and Warner-Lambert—have large plants in New Jersey. Food products, machinery, electronic equipment, and printed material are also manufactured in the state.

Even though New Jersey's official nickname is the Garden State, agriculture accounts for only 1 percent of its goods and services. Greenhouse and nursery products, such as flowers and shrubs, are New Jersey's most valuable source of farm income and are grown mostly in the northwest. This region is also home to many dairy farms. The southwestern part of the state boasts farm-fresh apples, peaches, tomatoes, peppers, and corn, while the Pinelands is known for its blueberries and cranberries. New Jersey ranks second in the nation in the production of blueberries and third in the production of cranberries.

New Jersey's coastal waters teem with fish and shellfish. Fishermen pull in flounder, sea bass, whiting, crabs, and oysters, but the big catch is clams. Two-thirds of the nation's clam harvest comes from New Jersey.

Chemical and drug manufacturing has been at the heart of New Jersey's industry for decades. Merck began operations in the state a century ago and continues to be a pillar of the economy today.

Dairy cows thrive on the velvety beds of grass found in the northwestern part of the state. Rich milk from New Jersey's dairy farms is shipped to nearby markets.

NO-COOK CRANBERRY RELISH

New Jersey is one of the nation's leading cranberry-producing states, and every October, people gather at the Chatsworth Cranberry Festival to celebrate New Jersey's cranberry harvest. With Pinelands musicians playing twangy tunes in the background, the crowd tours the cranberry bogs, eats cranberry muffins and cranberry sherbet, and drinks cranberry juice. Cranberry jelly and relish are sold to take home and enjoy later. The festival's highlight is a contest not only for the biggest cranberry but also for the smallest.

Have an adult help you make your own cranberry relish.

- 1 pound fresh cranberries (chopped coarsely—a food processor works well)
- 1 apple (chopped, with peel)
- 1 fresh orange (chopped, without peel)
- 1 small can of crushed pineapple
- ½ cup walnuts (chopped)
- ¾ cup granulated sugar
- 1 3-ounce package of strawberry or cherry gelatin

In a large bowl, dissolve the gelatin in one cup of hot water. Mix the remaining ingredients into the gelatin, stirring well. Refrigerate, and then enjoy!

New Jerseyans celebrate their seafood with festivals. During the summer, Atlantic City hosts the New Jersey Fresh Seafood Festival and Belmar hosts the New Jersey Seafood Festival. These events have something for everyone. With the Atlantic Ocean as a backdrop, children participate in races and games, local artists display their handmade crafts, and lively music echoes up and down the beach. But the real treat is sampling all the seafood. Steamed clams, fried fish and oysters, and boiled crabs are definite crowd pleasers.

COPING WITH HARD TIMES

New Jersey has seen its share of hard times. Camden was particularly hard hit in the late 1980s and early 1990s, when the two largest employers in the city, the Campbell Soup Company and General Electric, made major changes. Although Campbell's kept its headquarters in Camden, it moved its enormous soup manufacturing operation out of state. "It's still hard for me to talk about it," says Marna Robinson, who made soup for Campbell's for more than thirty years. "My whole life was Campbell's. The people I worked with and me, we were just like family and we loved our jobs. And then, boom!, the bottom dropped out. I work at a sandwich shop now, and it's just not the same."

Shortly thereafter, Campbell's next door neighbor, General Electric, cut more than three thousand workers, many of whom were electrical and aerospace engineers. "There were so many of us all looking for the same kind of work in the same vicinity that it was almost impossible to find a job in the field," says Dan Davis, an aerospace engineer. "I ended up working as a cashier in a variety store for almost two years before I finally found the engineering job I have now."

"It was really weird to go into the store and see my dad waiting on customers," says Dan's fifteen-year-old son, Bryan. "He was always worried about money. I used to go to bed at night and not be able to fall asleep because I was afraid we would end up homeless. I felt relieved when my dad got the job he has now, even though it meant we had to move across the state. It was hard

leaving all my friends, but I have new friends now and I'm pretty happy."

In the mid-1990s, telephone giant AT&T, located in Basking Ridge, also cut its workforce. Thousands of employees lost their jobs. Some were rehired after several months. Others were forced to learn new skills and begin new careers. Although New Jersey's workers have had to cope with many changes, most have found a way to pull through.

Although New Jersey has had its ups and downs in recent years, its future looks bright.

4 A MELTING POT

New Jersey's residents have roots all over the world. Almost 80 percent of New Jerseyans are the descendants of Europeans who came to farm the land, build canals and railroads, and work in factories.

African Americans account for about 13 percent of the population. New Jersey's first black residents were Africans who were brought to the colony as slaves. Later, blacks migrated to New Jersey from the southern states to work in factories. Today, blacks are coming from Caribbean nations such as Jamaica and Haiti.

Hispanics are a growing part of New Jersey's population. The number of Hispanics arriving from Puerto Rico, Cuba, and South America is on the rise. A smaller but significant percentage of New Jersey's residents are Asians, who have come from Vietnam, Japan, China, Korea, and India.

SUBURBS AND SMALL TOWNS

New Jersey's suburbs are home to thousands of people who commute into the cities to work. But for every person who commutes, there are many who do not. Lots of big city companies have moved their offices to the suburbs, and thousands of small businesses employ many thousands of people. Housing developments, shopping malls, and traffic congestion are the heart of many of New

Jersey's suburbs, and life tends to be hurried and hectic. "I do my grocery shopping late at night to avoid the crowds," says a woman who lives in a suburb of New York City. "I can't stand to fight for a parking place and then go in the store and wait in line." But in smaller communities, the pace is slower and neighbors take time to enjoy one another.

Festivals are held throughout New Jersey to celebrate the state's diverse cultures.

The farther reaches of the state are less populated and residents seem more laid back, although the once quiet coastal areas have seen amazing growth since the mid-1980s. Many young families and senior citizens have left cities in the northern part of the state to live year-round at the seashore. Lower housing prices and property taxes as well as low crime rates have attracted them. "We used to live in Paterson," says eleven-year-old John Ellio of Brick. "We lived in a duplex and we hardly had any yard at all. Here we have our own house and a nice yard. The best part is that my dad bought a boat for fishing. I love to fish!"

Most of the Pinelands is still rural. Towns are tiny, and traffic jams are unheard of. Residents pride themselves on keeping life simple and unhurried. Over the years, the people who live in the quietest areas have been known as pineys. Years ago, some made a living by gathering ferns, moss, and leaves of plants that grow in the Pinelands and selling them to flower shops to be used in floral arrangements. Others cut down cedar trees and sold the wood to boatbuilders. And many farmed blueberries and cranberries. Today, the children and grandchildren of the old-time pineys continue to rely on the land for their survival. "My family has lived here for generations," says a cranberry farmer, "and we wouldn't live any-where else. This land has been good to us. This is our home."

BIG CITIES

New Jersey's cities wrestle with the problems common in cities across the United States. Many of the factories and other businesses that once thrived in the cities have either shut down, moved to the

Living off the land has been the way of life for generations of cranberry farmers.

suburbs, or moved out of the state. With this change has come the loss of jobs for inner-city residents, followed by the dark cloud of poverty.

The change has also led to an epidemic of abandoned buildings. Over time, some of these crumbling buildings have become drug houses, where people gather to buy and use drugs. And where there are drugs, there are guns. Some inner-city children live in constant fear of being caught in gun crossfire. "My mama tells us to get down on the floor and crawl under a bed when we hear gunfire,"says a seven-year-old Newark girl.

But violence isn't the only problem. One Camden teenager says, "Our streets aren't just spoiled by violence, they're spoiled by pollution and garbage, too." In Camden and other cities, state funding is helping to correct some of these problems. Old, unsafe buildings have been knocked down, and new ones have been erected in their place. Some improvements are as simple as putting up street signs and making sure garbage is collected. A city's cleaner, brighter appearance can help encourage new businesses to establish there. And it is the new businesses that will bring money into the city and give jobs to its residents. In Camden, Mayor Milton Milan says,

New Jersey's cities are working hard to clean up their decaying neighborhoods. Progress is being made a step at a time.

THE JERSEY DEVIL: A PINELANDS LEGEND

Deep in the Pinelands on a stormy night in 1735, a woman struggled to give birth to her thirteenth child. Candlelight flickered against the bare walls indoors, while lightning darted through the black sky outdoors. With a final groan from the woman, a healthy baby boy emerged. But within seconds, its delicate human features gave way to gruesome monster features. With the body of a kangaroo, head of a dog, face of a horse, feet of a pig, tail of a serpent, and wings of a bat, the beast shot smoke from its nostrils, bellowed an eerie cry, and disappeared up the chimney and out into the darkness. And so began the legend of the Jersey Devil.

Over the years, droughts, crop failures, and fish diseases have been blamed on the creature. In January 1909, it supposedly spent a week terrorizing people from Camden to Trenton. Hundreds of people reported seeing the demon riding on wagons, killing animals, and breaking into homes. Afterward, it disappeared into the forest. In 1966, more than twenty ducks, geese, cats, and dogs were mysteriously killed on a farm in the heart of the Pinelands. Was it the work of the Jersey Devil? Just ask a New Jerseyan!

"Camden is open for business!" And he even erected a billboard saying so!

CELEBRATING DIVERSITY

Not all is bad in New Jersey's cities. Some of the state's best performing arts theaters, museums, and art galleries are found there. And New Jersey's cities are bubbling with ethnic culture. Many city restaurants, especially in the northern and central regions of the state, cater to the tastes of their customers. Restaurants in Newark please the city's large Portuguese-American population by serving traditional Portuguese dishes. "My favorite dish is rabbit with rice, and you don't find that in just any restaurant," says Antonio Penedo, a native of Portugal.

Trenton boasts an Italian district, where restaurants serve lasagna, tortellini, ziti, meatballs, and, of course, pizza. More than two million New Jerseyans are of Italian descent.

New Jersey's residents of Irish and German descent enjoy annual

Children in costume enjoy a Portuguese celebration in Newark, where a large number of Portuguese Americans live.

ETHNIC NEW JERSEY

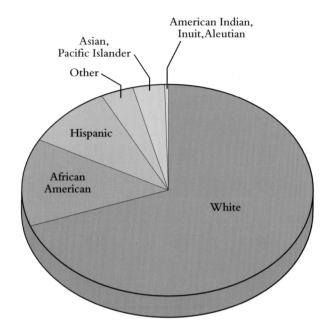

American Indian, Inuit, Aleutian

Asian, Pacific Islander

Other

Hispanic

African American

White

festivities to celebrate their heritage. Traditional Irish music and wearing green are highlights of the St. Patrick's Day parade in Seaside Heights, while yodelers and German food, such as sauerbraten and Wiener schnitzel, are highlights of Oktoberfest in Stanhope and Little Egg Harbor.

Many immigrants from the Caribbean, especially Haiti, have chosen East and West Orange as their new home. Foods made from guava and papaya sell well, and hot Haitian bread is a favorite. Many residents of Perth Amboy have come from Central and South America. More than half of the city's population speaks Spanish at home.

Edgewater's large Asian population is reflected in the Yoahan U.S.A. Corp., a unique Asian shopping center. Stores and restau-

A man in Fort Lee prepares eel, a traditional Japanese dish.

rants offer Japanese, Chinese, and Korean products and foods. In Edison, Woodbridge, and Iselin, it is not unusual to see Indian-American women dressed in saris, the native dress of India. These long, flowing dresses are made of beautiful, brightly colored fabric.

Although few Native Americans live in New Jersey today, Native American culture is celebrated in Belvidere at the Return to Beaver Creek Powwow. Dancers in beaded costumes and jewelry perform to the beat of Indian music, while talented artists display their most elaborate creations.

A RELIGIOUS MIX

With the ethnic mix of New Jersey's residents also comes a religious mix. Catholics, Protestants, Jews, Hindus, Muslims, Buddhists, and others are the people of New Jersey. During the 1600s, the Dutch set up their Reformed Church, and the English established Puritan and Quaker settlements. Presbyterians, Lutherans, and Methodists arrived in the 1700s. In 1848, Jews established New Jersey's first synagogue in Newark.

The first Roman Catholic parish was established in 1814. So many Catholics emigrated from Ireland in the mid-1800s and from Italy in the late 1800s that the number of Catholics in New Jersey soared. Today, they are the state's largest religious group.

In Italy, Catholics celebrate the Feast of Our Lady of Mount Carmel on July 16 in honor of the Virgin Mary. When Italian immigrants arrived in America in the 1800s, many settled in the Hammonton area. They continued the tradition of celebrating the feast day on July 16. In time, the celebration in Hammonton became bigger and attracted thousands of worshipers from all over. Masses, parades, and fireworks marked the occasion. Catholics still gather in Hammonton every summer to celebrate this special day.

FAVORITE PASTIMES

Regardless of their ethnic or religious backgrounds, New Jerseyans eagerly gather to take part in sports and cheer for their favorite teams.

Crowds throng to the Meadowlands to watch football, basketball, and ice hockey. Avid fans support the New York Jets and Giants of the National Football League (who make New Jersey their home), the Nets of the National Basketball Association, and the Devils (named after the Jersey Devil) of the National Hockey League. Baseball fans are not left out, either. Elsewhere in the state,

Football fans pack Giants Stadium at the Meadowlands.

Young people learn to ride and groom horses at the many stables located throughout New Jersey.

minor league games are played by the Trenton Thunder and the New Jersey Cardinals of Augusta.

In Atlantic City, boxing draws crowds. Tickets sell quickly for seats at the casino hotels, which host championship fights.

Horseback riding and horse racing are important to New Jerseyans, who claim the horse as their state animal. The United States Equestrian Team even chose Gladstone, New Jersey, as its training center. Riding stables in small towns throughout the state

NEW JERSEY STATE FAIR

For one magical week in August, New Jerseyans gather at the state fair in Cherry Hill. A petting zoo delights young children, while dime tosses and dart throws excite older ones. Plump pigs and brawny bulls are up for inspection, along with sleek horses, the state animal. New Jerseyans have had a long love affair with horseback riding and horse racing.

Incubators lined with baby chicks hatching from eggs remind visitors of the poultry industry that has been a part of New Jersey's economy through the years. In celebration of the state's dairy industry, there are cows to be milked.

Lines are long for favorite foods, such as the cheesesteaks and soft pretzels that nearby Philadelphia sends across the Delaware River. "But funnel cake is my weakness," says Stefanie Volkmann of the Greater Cherry Hill Chamber of Commerce. "And I always eat too much!" Funnel cake was originated more than two hundred years ago by Dutch farm families. The Dutch were among New Jersey's first European settlers.

offer riding lessons and host horse shows. "When I was eleven, I rode a horse named Chocolate in a horse show at the Woodedge Stables and I won the blue ribbon," says Beverly Tadeu, a forty-year-old who continues to ride horses for pleasure. "That day still stands out in my mind as one of the most exciting days of my life." Racetracks throughout the state offer fans the thrill of watching harness and thoroughbred racing.

Recreational sports are also popular. Boating, swimming, and saltwater fishing in the Atlantic Ocean and Barnegat Bay are favorites on summer weekends. Inland, New Jerseyans spend time canoeing and freshwater fishing in lakes and streams. Hot-air ballooning and plane gliding are becoming more and more popular, especially in the northwestern region of the state. And endless nature trails in New Jersey's many state parks lure hikers and bicyclists during spring, summer, and fall, while ski slopes draw crowds through the winter. No matter what the season, New Jerseyans can enjoy the outdoors.

Bicycling along peaceful back roads is a popular weekend sport.

5 OUTSTANDING NEW JERSEYANS

New Jerseyans have made their mark in every field, and many have touched the lives of young people. Some were born in New Jersey, while others chose to live and work there later in life.

ENTERTAINMENT

People across the country are awed by the amazing talent of magician David Copperfield, who was born in Metuchen. Taking magic a step beyond, Copperfield is so clever that he has been featured on many television specials, which are filmed before live audiences. One of his most incredible feats was making a jet airplane disappear before his fans' eyes.

Jack Nicholson is one of Hollywood's greatest actors, famous for his menacing demeanor and wicked grin. Although he has won Academy Awards for other films, Nicholson is best known among young people for playing the evil Joker in the movie *Batman*. Nicholson was born in Neptune.

Whitney Houston of Newark is a popular singer and actor. Her smooth songs such as "I Will Always Love You" have often reached the top of music charts, and her compact discs have sold millions of copies. She has also appeared in such popular films as *The Bodyguard* and *Waiting to Exhale*.

Frank Sinatra, who was born in Hoboken, was one of the world's

"I've been to other magic shows, but nobody's as good as David Copperfield," says one fan.

The daughter of a gospel singer, Whitney Houston began her own singing career with a gospel choir when she was only eleven years old. As a teenager, she sang backup for popular rhythm-and-blues singers Chaka Khan and Lou Rawls.

most popular singers. He was a crowd pleaser at the casinos in Atlantic City over the years, and he starred in several movies, earning an Academy Award for his performance in *From Here to Eternity*. Sinatra's twinkling blue eyes led to his nickname, Old Blue Eyes.

Bruce Springsteen is considered one of the most dynamic performers in rock music. For many people, he represents the spirit of working-class New Jersey. The words to his songs echo the struggles and dreams of everyday people. Born and raised in Freehold, Spring-

In addition to being a talented singer and guitarist, Bruce Springsteen is also a gifted songwriter.

THERE SHE IS . . .

"There she is . . . Miss America!" These familiar words bring to mind the spectacle that takes place in Atlantic City each September. Since 1921, the resort has been home to the Miss America Pageant.

The pageant began because an enterprising hotel owner, H. Conrad Eckholm, hated to see the summer tourist season end. To keep the crowds in town a little bit longer, Eckholm held a parade featuring beautiful young ladies. Although the first parade flaunted only seven women, Eckholm's plan worked. Tourists stayed in town to watch, and they looked forward to another parade the following year. And so began a long-standing tradition.

The pageant now includes a representative from each of the fifty states and the District of Columbia. A parade is still held, but it takes place before the night of the pageant. Today, millions of viewers tune in to watch the pageant on television.

When the pageant began, beauty was everything, but these days, looks alone are not enough to win the crown. Talent, personality, and strength of character are also important. Miss America is now both a role model and a celebrity.

steen got his start by playing in nightspots along the Asbury Park boardwalk. In 1993, Springsteen won an Academy Award for his song "Streets of Philadelphia" from the motion picture *Philadelphia*.

ART AND LITERATURE

Charles Addams gained fame for drawing a magazine cartoon of a strange and spooky family named Addams. His cartoon became so popular that a television series called *The Addams Family* was based on his unusual characters. Later, these characters became the focus of the humorous *Addams Family* movies, which have delighted young people across the country. Addams was born in Westfield.

Probably no New Jersey writer is so familiar to young people as author Judy Blume, who was born in Elizabeth. Her books, such

Although Judy Blume is most famous for her children's books, she has also written successful novels for adults, including Smart Women.

Amiri Baraka first gained fame in the 1960s for his powerful plays about relations between blacks and whites.

as *Blubber* and *Are You There God? It's Me, Margaret*, speak to the hearts of young people. Her young fans feel that she really understands what their lives are like.

Poet William Carlos Williams was born in Rutherford, New Jersey, and left his hometown only to go to school in Philadelphia, where he earned his medical degree. Williams returned to Rutherford to set up a doctor's office. Before and after work, he wrote sensitive poetry about the people and events he came across in his life. *Paterson*, one of Williams's important long poems, is about Paterson, New Jersey.

Another outstanding New Jerseyan, Amiri Baraka, is both a poet and a playwright. In plays such as *Dutchman* and *The Slave*, Baraka wrote about the harshness of inner-city life and the injustices faced by African Americans. Baraka continues to live in his hometown of Newark.

POLITICS

Two U.S. presidents had connections to New Jersey. Grover Cleveland was born in Caldwell. He was the only president to serve two terms that did not come one immediately after the other. This made him both the twenty-second and twenty-fourth president. He was also the only president to get married while in the White House. After his retirement, Cleveland returned to New Jersey to live in Princeton, where he taught at Princeton University.

Grover Cleveland is the only U.S. president to be elected to nonconsecutive terms. He served from 1885 to 1889 and again from 1893 to 1897.

Woodrow Wilson was born in Virginia but came to New Jersey to attend Princeton University. Later, he began teaching at Princeton and became the university's president in 1902. In 1910, Wilson was elected governor of New Jersey. Two years later, he was elected president of the United States. As president, Wilson guided America through World War I. He also promoted an international peace organization called the League of Nations. Wilson won the Nobel Peace Prize in 1920.

SCIENCE AND MEDICINE

Princeton, New Jersey, is home to Princeton University, the state's oldest university and one of the nation's most prestigious. It is also home to the Institute for Advanced Study. Over the years, these institutions have attracted many brilliant scholars from all over the world. But perhaps none was so famous—or so brilliant—as German-born physicist Albert Einstein. By the time Einstein moved to Princeton to work at the Institute for Advanced Study in the early 1930s, his revolutionary theories about how the universe works had already earned him the Nobel Prize in physics. Einstein once said, "I have no special gift—I am only passionately curious." Einstein remained in Princeton until his death in 1955.

Another world-renowned scientist who worked in New Jersey was Thomas Edison, whose discoveries changed the world. He is most famous for inventing the phonograph and the first practical electric light, and for developing motion pictures. But in all he came up with more than a thousand inventions. Edison once said that his mission in life was "to do everything in [his] power to further free the people

Albert Einstein is often called the Father of Relativity. His research in physics led to the equation for which he is so famous: $E=mc^2$.

from drudgery and create the largest possible measure of happiness and prosperity."

Although not a household name like Einstein or Edison, medical researcher Selman Waksman also contributed much to humanity. Born in the Ukraine, Waksman came to the United States as a young man. While studying at Rutgers University in New Jersey, Waksman became fascinated by a tiny organism called the actinomycete, which lives in the soil. After earning a doctorate at the University of California, Waksman began teaching at Rutgers, where he continued doing research on the actinomycete. In 1943, he discovered that a medicine called streptomycin could be produced from the organism. Streptomycin was able to cure tuberculosis, blood poisoning, and certain diseases of the bladder and kidneys. Countless lives were saved because of Waksman's discovery, and he won the Nobel Prize in medicine in 1952.

AVIATION

Astronaut Edwin Eugene Aldrin Jr., known as Buzz, was born in Montclair. He became an astronaut in 1963, after receiving his doctorate in astronautics from the Massachusetts Institute of

Apollo 11 commander Neil Armstrong took this picture of Edwin "Buzz" Aldrin standing on front of the lunar module during their historic moon walk on July 20, 1969.

NEW JERSEY AND AVIATION

New Jersey has played an important role in the history of American aviation. In 1793, Frenchman Jean-Pierre Blanchard made America's first airborne trip when he traveled from Philadelphia, Pennsylvania, to Deptford, New Jersey, in a balloon. At the end of his fifteen-mile journey, he brought the balloon down on open farmland. Blanchard presented astonished farmers with a letter from George Washington asking that they extend to him "humanity and good will which may render honour to their country," which they did.

More than one hundred years later, when airplane travel was in its infancy, the Wright Aeronautical Corporation began manufacturing airplane engines in Paterson. A Wright engine powered Charles Lindbergh's plane, the *Spirit of St. Louis*, when Lindbergh made his famous solo flight from New York to Paris in 1927. Lindbergh lived in Hopewell, New Jersey. The following year, Amelia Earhart became the first woman to fly over the Atlantic Ocean, when she rode a plane built by Fokker, another New Jersey company.

During the same period, Lakehurst became a base for dirigibles, or airships. The *Shenandoah* became the first dirigible to fly across the country when it journeyed from Lakehurst to San Diego, California, in 1924. By the early 1930s, Germany was flying dirigibles across the Atlantic Ocean and landing them in Lakehurst. But on May 6, 1937, the German airship *Hindenburg* burned in midair as it attempted to land at Lakehurst. Thirty-six of the ninety-seven people aboard were killed, ending the era of dirigible air travel from Germany. Lakehurst's dirigible program ended completely in 1961. Hangar No. 1, which had housed the enormous airships, was made a National Historic Landmark in 1968.

Technology. He piloted the *Gemini 12* spaceflight in 1966. During the flight, he left the spacecraft and "walked" in space. His walk, which actually involved doing work outside the spacecraft while being attached to it with a lifeline, lasted five and one-half hours and proved that people could work outside an orbiting vehicle. On July 20, 1969, when the *Apollo 11* lunar module landed on the moon, Aldrin followed Neil Armstrong out of the module, becoming the second person ever to set foot on the moon.

SPORTS

Track star Carl Lewis is one of New Jersey's best-known athletes. Although he was born in Alabama, he grew up in Willingboro, New Jersey. Lewis dominated the 1984 summer Olympics, winning four gold medals—in the 100- and 200-meter dashes, the 400-meter relay, and the long jump. Lewis stayed at the top of his field for a remarkably long time. He won four straight Olympic gold medals in the long jump, earning his last one at the 1996 games, before he finally retired.

6 A GARDEN STATE TOUR

OWNFEST '94
300 Strolling Clowns
PT 24–25
ARADE &
IRCUS

MOTO
CYCLE

Every region in New Jersey is filled with interesting places. The state has as much to offer its own residents as it does its visitors from around the world.

NORTHERN NEW JERSEY

Jersey City is the home of Liberty State Park, which overlooks the Statue of Liberty. Visitors can travel by ferry to see the giant statue and Ellis Island, where millions of immigrants first set foot on U.S. shores. Back on the mainland, the Liberty Science Center is filled with hands-on exhibits, such as the Touch Tunnel, a tunnel of complete darkness that visitors must navigate by feeling their way with their hands. The Bug Zoo is another popular display. "I got a chance to watch bees and ants and even some tarantulas up close," says nine-year-old Christopher Hawkins. "I want to be an entomologist when I grow up."

African-American history is highlighted at the Afro-American Historical Society Museum in Jersey City. Exhibits cover a full range of African-American history and culture, from the civil rights movement to African sculpture and musical instruments. There is even a fascinating display of black dolls. At the African Art Museum in Tenafly, a little farther north, African masks, statues, crafts, and textiles are exhibited.

From Liberty State Park, visitors can see the Statue of Liberty, America's premier symbol of freedom, and Ellis Island, the landing place of millions of immigrants who arrived in search of the American dream.

Also clustered in the state's northeastern corner is Newark, New Jersey's largest city. Amid Newark's tall buildings and bustling streets is Branch Brook Park, which has more than two thousand cherry trees. Hundreds of thousands of visitors gather to admire these trees during the Cherry Blossom Festival every April. Nearby is the Catholic Basilica of the Sacred Heart, an architectural wonder that took fifty-six years to build. Groundbreaking took place in 1898, but the huge Roman Catholic church was not completed until 1954. The building is noted for its soaring towers and pointed arches, but most famous are its spectacular stained-glass windows, which are considered among the most magnificent in the world.

Antique clocks, rare coins, and early American quilts are some of the treasures found at the Newark Museum. The museum's Native American Gallery features costumes, jewelry, and tools of America's first people.

In the 1600s, some Lenni Lenape lived in a village near present-day Stanhope. During the 1700s, the site was a busy ironworks named Andover Forge. With the industrial boom of the 1800s, Andover Forge became Waterloo Village, a bustling town. Today, restored buildings and a museum showcase the area's rich history. Craftspeople demonstrating early American trades bring to life what it was like to be a gunsmith, a potter, or a broom maker. A re-created 1625 Lenni Lenape village, complete with wigwams and furnished longhouses, also stands on the site.

Morristown National Historic Park preserves the site where George Washington and his troops spent the winter of 1779–1780. While Washington stayed at the comfortable home of Mrs. Jacob Ford Jr., his men stayed four miles away at Jockey Hollow. Wash-

At Waterloo Village, a craftsman demonstrates broom making. In colonial days, skilled craftsmen such as blacksmiths, wheelwrights, shoemakers, and weavers made items by hand because there were no machines to do these jobs.

ington's men chopped down acres of surrounding forest to build huts for shelter from the coldest winter in a century. With one snowstorm after another preventing food supplies from reaching them, the men came near starvation. Tempe Wick, a young girl who lived nearby, is said to have feared that her horse would be eaten by the starving soldiers, so she hid him in her bedroom for safety! Today, the park includes the Ford mansion and the Wick house,

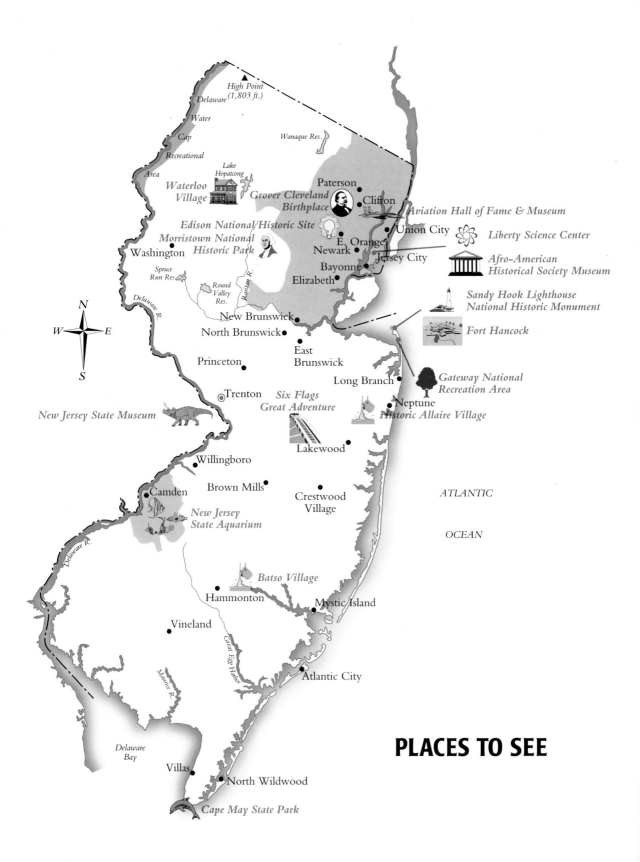

High Point
(1,803 ft.)

Delaware

Water

Cap

Recreational

Area

Wanaque Res.

Lake
Hopatcong

Waterloo
Village

Grover Cleveland
Birthplace

Paterson

Clifton

Aviation Hall of Fame & Museum

Edison National Historic Site

Union City

Liberty Science Center

Morristown National
Historic Park

E. Orange

Newark

Jersey City

Afro-American
Historical Society Museum

Washington

Bayonne

Sandy Hook Lighthouse
National Historic Monument

Spruce
Run Res.

Round
Valley
Res.

Elizabeth

Fort Hancock

Delaware R.

Rappahan R.

New Brunswick

North Brunswick

N

East
Brunswick

W   E

S

Princeton

Trenton

Long Branch

Gateway National
Recreation Area

New Jersey State Museum

Six Flags
Great Adventure

Neptune

Historic Allaire Village

Lakewood

Willingboro

Brown Mills

Crestwood
Village

ATLANTIC

Camden

OCEAN

New Jersey
State Aquarium

Delaware R.

Batso Village

Hammonton

Mystic Island

Vineland

Great Egg Harbor R.

Maurice R.

Atlantic City

Delaware
Bay

Villas

North Wildwood

Cape May State Park

PLACES TO SEE

where visitors can see the little bedroom in which Tempe Wick hid her horse. A few log huts have been reconstructed to show how the soldiers lived during that terrible winter.

The laboratories where Thomas Edison made his great inventions are located in Menlo Park and West Orange. The Thomas Edison Memorial Tower (shaped like a lightbulb on top) and Museum in Menlo Park mark the spot where Edison invented the phonograph and perfected the electric light. In West Orange, Edison's mansion, called Glenmont, and the laboratory where he developed moving pictures have been preserved at the Edison National Historic Site.

Teterboro Airport is home to the Aviation Hall of Fame and Museum of New Jersey. Bronze plaques honor New Jerseyans who have made aviation history, including Charles Lindbergh and Buzz Aldrin. Aircraft, jet engines, and even rocket engines are also on display.

CENTRAL NEW JERSEY

The state capitol in Trenton is the second-oldest capitol building in continuous use in the United States. New Jersey lawmakers have been meeting there since 1792. Visitors today admire its dome covered in twenty-three-karat gold leaf.

The New Jersey State Museum in Trenton is notable for its display of New Jersey–made pottery and glass, but its most impressive exhibit is *Hadrosaurus foulkii*, the first dinosaur skeleton found in the United States. In 1838, a farmer in Haddonfield came upon some very large bones while digging on his land. He did not know they were dinosaur bones. Twenty years later, when he met a scientist and told him about the bones, he finally found out how great his discovery had been. The scientist wasted no time in having the remaining bones dug up. Over the years, scientists have learned that the creature had a birdlike jaw and walked on its hind legs while using its front legs to search for food. Its posture resembled that of a modern bird. Today, a plaque at the site where the bones were found honors the farmer's fabulous discovery.

In Camden, the Thomas H. Kean New Jersey State Aquarium gives visitors a chance to examine underwater life ranging from sea turtles to some very freaky-looking fish. "I even got to pet a baby shark," says ten-year-old Erin Schonewolf. "Its skin felt just like sandpaper!"

Rutgers, which was chartered as Queen's College in 1766, is the second-oldest university in New Jersey. At the New Brunswick campus is the Rutgers Geology Museum, which features fossils and the skeleton of a mastodon, an extinct giant mammal similar to an elephant.

Allaire Village, in Monmouth County, was an early 1800s iron-works where pots and kettles and the pipes for New York City's waterworks were made. Tourists can visit the restored Historic Allaire Village and marvel at the huge beehive-shaped stack that remains of the original furnace.

The Howell Living History Farm in Titusville gives visitors a chance to see what farm life was like in New Jersey as the 1800s folded into the 1900s. Visitors can watch horse-drawn haying, harvesting, and cultivating, and even maple sugaring and sheep shearing. Historic Longstreet Farm in Holmdel also gives visitors a chance to look back in time. Not only do farmhands milk cows by

The Thomas H. Kean New Jersey State Aquarium is the gem of the Camden waterfront. Inside, marine life fascinates visitors of all ages.

hand and use old-fashioned combines to work the fields, but they also dress in the style of the late 1800s.

Farther south, in Jackson, the Six Flags Great Adventure Park offers a drive-through safari. Lions, tigers, zebras, baboons, and ostriches are just some of the wildlife living freely there. The ostriches walk right up to the cars and peck on the windows, and some baboons are so bold that they ride on the roofs!

SOUTHERN NEW JERSEY

Southern New Jersey is filled with history. The first log cabin built in the United States is in Gibbstown. The Nothnagle Log House was built by Swedish settlers in the mid-1600s.

Batsto Iron Works in the Pinelands was a hub of the bog iron industry from the 1760s through the 1830s. During the Revolutionary War, cannonballs and other munitions were made there. Later, the glassmaking industry took hold, but eventually, Batsto was abandoned and left to deteriorate. In 1954, the state purchased the land and began to restore the village. Today, small wooden houses are lined up side by side just as they were over a century ago when iron- and glassworkers lived in them. They contrast sharply with the grand mansion where the owner lived. Visitors can also visit a general store and a craft and pottery house and imagine what life was like in this forested village long ago.

The Bridgeton area boasts the state's largest historic district, with more than two thousand historic homes, churches, and public buildings dating back to the 1700s and 1800s. The Nail House Museum was once part of a thriving nail factory. Today, the building houses a display of antique toys, dolls, and glass and pottery made in New Jersey. Nearby is the Woodruff Indian Museum, which showcases thousands of Native American artifacts. At the Nanticoke Lenape Village, wigwams and a ceremonial longhouse have been recreated.

The Wheaton Museum of American Glass in Millville showcases some of the extraordinary glassware made in this country since colonial times.

In Millville, where glassmaking has prospered since the early 1800s, visitors can tour Wheaton Village. Many years ago, the fragile work of making glass was done by hand by skilled craftsmen, but today, most of the work is done by machinery. A re-created factory at Wheaton Village features glassblowers at work. They make lovely vases, pitchers, and paperweights. A real treat are the wondrous displays at the Wheaton Museum of American Glass.

Old medicine bottles, paperweights, baby bottles, fruit jars, and ink wells are just a few of the many items featured.

Rodeo lovers do not have to leave New Jersey to experience the thrill of the real thing. The Cowtown Rodeo, the oldest and largest rodeo on the East Coast, takes place in Woodstown, near Salem, from May through September. In the 1920s Woodstown was the site of a county fair and auction. Stony Harris, the auctioneer, thought it would be fun to hold a rodeo, and the idea caught on. Today, the best cowboys and cowgirls from around the country dazzle spectators with bronco riding, bull riding, and calf roping.

COASTAL NEW JERSEY

The Sandy Hook Lighthouse National Historic Landmark was first lit in 1764. The white, 103-foot-tall, eight-sided lighthouse was built because many ships met with disaster while trying to enter the New York Harbor. The tower has been lit ever since, making it the oldest lighthouse in use in the United States.

Also at Sandy Hook is Fort Hancock, which was completed in 1895. For many years, the army used the fort to defend New York Harbor, but today it houses a museum that displays military artifacts and old photographs.

At the Gateway National Recreation Area at Sandy Hook, visitors can enjoy swimming and canoeing as well as nature walks through a natural holly forest. The forest is the oldest and largest wild holly forest on the East Coast.

While many visitors to the Jersey shore take in historic sites, they spend most of their time simply relaxing on the beach and swimming in the ocean. Long Branch became famous for being the favorite vacation spot of United States presidents from the 1860s through the early 1900s. The town still lures vacationers with its cool summer breezes and refreshing ocean waves.

In the 1860s, Ocean Grove also began to lure vacationers, and by the 1890s, thousands of people flocked to the seaside resort each summer. In 1894, a huge wooden auditorium was built there.

Ocean Grove began as a religious seaside resort in 1869, with vacationers living in tents during their stay. In time, small wooden cottages replaced the tents, and finally lovely Victorian homes replaced the cottages.

OLD BARNEY

Among New Jersey's most famous landmarks is the red-and-white Barnegat Lighthouse, nicknamed Old Barney, which stands at the mouth of Barnegat Inlet. Old Barney began service in 1859 after replacing a forty-foot brick tower. The lighthouse warned passing ships of dangerous shoals until its retirement in 1927, when a lightship anchored eight miles offshore took over its duties.

Old Barney later served as a lookout tower for the coast guard during World War II. After the war, the state took over the lighthouse and eventually turned the site into the Barnegat Lighthouse State Park.

Standing 165 feet tall, Old Barney is the tallest of New Jersey's lighthouses. It is also one of the most photographed lighthouses in the country. Visitors may climb the 217 steps to the top for a spectacular view of Long Beach Island, the Barnegat Bay, and the Atlantic Ocean.

Ocean Grove is still popular with vacationers, who often enjoy the concerts held in the Great Auditorium.

Lucy, the Margate Elephant, was an unusual attraction when she was built in Margate in 1881, and she remains so. Lucy is sixty-five feet tall and was originally made of wood covered with tin. Over the years, she has withstood storms, fire, and a short move. She

Ocean fishing at Island Beach State Park is especially appealing at sunrise. "My grandpop and I like to fish when we have the beach all to ourselves," says a young visitor. "I like to listen to the rhythm of the surf while I fish."

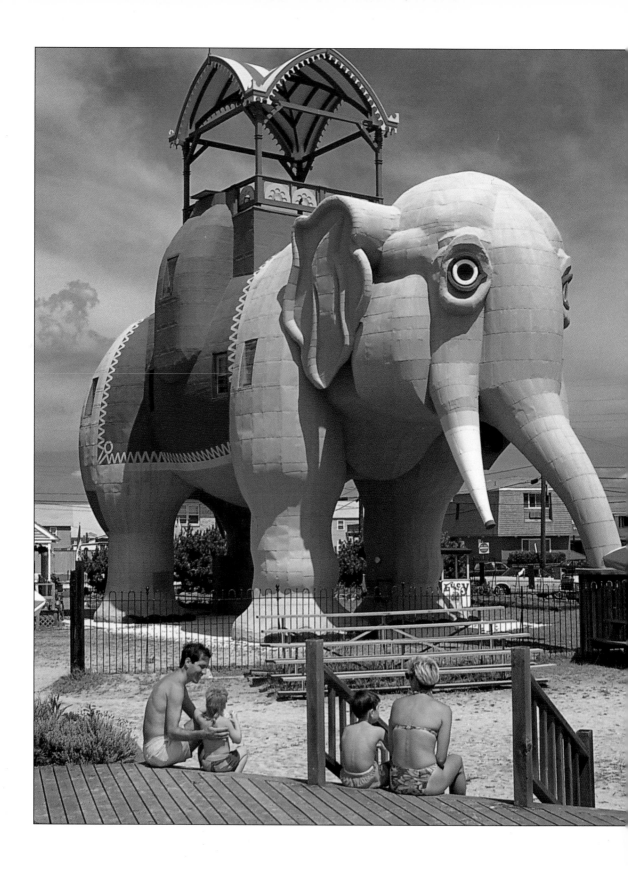

was restored in the 1970s and got a new steel frame. Lucy has served as a real estate office, a tourist attraction, a house, and, finally, a museum. In 1977, she was made a National Historic Landmark. Visitors can climb the stairs in her hind legs to tour a small museum in her belly, and then climb out onto an observation deck for a fine view of the surrounding area. "I remember my parents driving us down the shore to see Lucy when I was a little girl," says Lori Knopf, who now lives in Delaware. "And now here I am with my children!"

Atlantic City, New Jersey's most popular resort, offers something for everyone, from swimming in the ocean to strolling the boardwalk to gambling in the casinos. The world's first boardwalk was laid at Atlantic City in 1870. Jacob Keim, a hotel owner, and Alexander Boardman, a train conductor, came up with the idea to prevent visitors from tracking sand from the beach into hotels and train cars. The first saltwater taffy was made here in the 1880s. When Charles Darrow invented the popular board game Monopoly in 1930, he named the streets in the game after the actual streets in Atlantic City, his favorite resort.

Cape May, considered the nation's oldest seaside resort, lies at the southernmost tip of New Jersey. In colonial days, New Jerseyans and Philadelphians enjoyed Cape May's beaches and breezes. By the 1840s, Cape May was luring summer vacationers from all over. During the final decades of the 1800s, ornate mansions were built in Cape May, and many still stand today. The mansions are

A trip to the Jersey shore would not be complete without a stop in Margate to see Lucy. She has dazzled tourists for over a century.

BIRDS LOVE CAPE MAY

The Cape May area is a wonderful bird haven. More than four hundred species of birds have been recorded in this region, making it one of the best bird-watching sites in all of North America.

Cape May Point State Park is both the year-round home of many species and a stop for migrating birds that pass through the area. Particularly spectacular is the hawk migration that takes place in autumn. From early September though late November, hundreds of hawks can be seen each day. Some of the species sighted include red-shouldered hawks, northern goshawks, and peregrine falcons. Bird lovers from all over gather for the annual Cape May Hawk Watch, a hike through the area in search of hawks.

celebrated in October during Victorian Week, when they are open for touring, and in December during Christmas in Cape May, when they are decorated for Christmas and carolers dress in nineteenth-century costumes.

In the 1600s and 1700s, before Cape May became a seaside resort, it was a whaling town. Cape May whale oil and whalebone were well-known products in the colonies. Although the whaling industry no longer exists in Cape May, many visitors enjoy taking whale-watching cruises. Besides offering a peek at the magnificent creatures, these excursions also provide a view of the beautiful New Jersey coast.

THE FLAG: *The flag, which was adopted in 1896, is a colored version of the seal set against a yellow background.*

THE SEAL: *In the center of the state seal is a shield picturing three plows, which represent agriculture. The horse's head above the shield symbolizes speed, strength, and agriculture. Flanking the shield are goddesses representing liberty and agriculture. The state seal was adopted in 1928.*

STATE SURVEY

Statehood: December 18, 1787

Origin of Name: Named after the island of Jersey in the English Channel

Nickname: Garden State

Capital: Trenton

Motto: Liberty and Prosperity

Bird: Eastern goldfinch

Flower: Purple violet

Tree: Red oak

Insect: Honeybee

Animal: Horse

Fish: Brook trout

Violet

Red oak

IN NEW JERSEY

New Jersey has no official state song. The lyrics to this song were written in 1994 by fourth graders in the Van Holten Elementary School in Bridgewater under the direction of their teachers Carol Forte, Diane Silverster, and Sandy Vitale. It is under consideration for adoption as the state song.

Colors: Buff and blue

Folk dance: Square dance

Dinosaur: *Hadrosaurus foulkii*

Shell: Knobbed whelk

GEOGRAPHY

Highest Point: 1,803 feet above sea level, at High Point

Lowest Point: sea level along the Atlantic coast

Area: 7,790 square miles

Greatest Distance, North to South: 167 miles

Greatest Distance, East to West: 88 miles

Bordering States: New York to the north and east, Pennsylvania to the west, Delaware to the southwest

Hottest Recorded Temperature: 110°F at Runyon on July 10, 1936

Coldest Recorded Temperature: -34°F at River Vale on January 5, 1904

Average Annual Precipitation: 45 inches

Major Rivers: Delaware, Great Egg Harbor, Hackensack, Hudson, Maurice, Millstone, Passaic, Raritan

Major Lakes: Budd, Culver, Green Pond, Greenwood, Hopatcong, Mohawk, Swartswood

Trees: beech, birch, cedar, maple, oak, pitch pine, short-leaf pine, sweet gum, yellow poplar

Wild Plants: azalea, buttercup, goldenrod, honeysuckle, mountain laurel, purple violet, Queen Anne's lace, rhododendron, Virginia cowslip

Animals: deer, fox, mink, muskrat, opossum, otter, rabbit, raccoon, skunk

Birds: blue jay, cardinal, duck, goldfinch, goose, partridge, pheasant, robin, ruffed grouse, sandpiper, wild turkey

Fish: bass, bluefish, clam, crappie, menhaden, oyster, pickerel, pike, salmon, shad, sturgeon, trout, weakfish

Endangered Animals: American peregrine falcon, bald eagle, bog turtle, Indiana bat, northeastern beach tiger beetle, piping plover, roseate tern

Endangered Plants: American chaffseed, Knieskern's beaked-rush, sensitive joint-vetch, small whorled pogonia, swamp pink

Small whorled pogonia

TIMELINE

New Jersey History

1500s The Lenni Lenape live in the area that will become New Jersey

1524 Giovanni da Verrazano explores the New Jersey coast

1609 Henry Hudson explores the Sandy Hook Bay area

1660 Dutch settlers found Bergen, New Jersey's first permanent European settlement

1664 The English gain control of New Jersey

1666 Newark is founded

1746 Princeton University is founded

1750 New Jersey's first public library is established in Trenton

1774 Colonists in Greenwich burn a supply of British tea to protest British taxes

1775 The American Revolution begins

1776 George Washington and his troops cross the Delaware River on Christmas night to stage a surprise attack at the Battle of Trenton

1787 New Jersey becomes the third state

1790 Trenton is named New Jersey's capital

1804 Vice President Aaron Burr kills Alexander Hamilton in a duel at Weehawken

1817 The state legislature establishes a public school system

1858 The first dinosaur skeleton found in North America is discovered in Haddonfield

1861–1865 The Civil War

1879 Thomas Edison perfects the lightbulb in Menlo Park

1884 Grover Cleveland becomes the only native New Jerseyan elected president

1912 New Jersey governor Woodrow Wilson is elected president

1919 The first regularly scheduled air passenger service in the United States begins between Atlantic City and New York City

1937 The German dirigible *Hindenburg* explodes over Lakehurst, killing 36 people

1947 New Jersey adopts its present constitution

1952 The New Jersey Turnpike opens

1967 A riot in Newark leaves 26 dead and more than 1,000 injured

1978 Casino gambling begins in Atlantic City

1994 Christine Todd Whitman becomes New Jersey's first female governor

ECONOMY

Agricultural Products: beans, blueberries, corn, cranberries, greenhouse and nursery plants, milk, peaches, potatoes, soybeans, tomatoes

Natural Resources: clams, clay, crushed stone, fish, sand and gravel

Clams

Manufactured Products: chemicals, electrical equipment, food products, machinery, pharmaceuticals, printed materials, scientific instruments

Business and Trade: insurance, real estate, research laboratories, transportation, wholesale and retail trade

CALENDAR OF CELEBRATIONS

Super Science Weekend Each January the New Jersey State Museum in Trenton sponsors a celebration of science and technology. You can take part in science experiments, watch special planetarium shows, and hear scientists talk about their work.

Cherry Blossom Festival A half million people visit Newark's Branch Brook Park each April to admire the spectacular blossoms of the park's 2,700 cherry trees.

Shad Festival Each April Lambertville celebrates the shad that migrate up the Delaware River. Thousands of people come to enjoy tastes of such fishy dishes as shad cakes, shad gumbo, smoked shad, and shad salad. The event also features storytelling, music, and a dance.

Whitesbog Blueberry Festival A running race through the Pinelands kicks off this June event in Browns Mills. Afterward, children can make crafts, play games, and even go on a hayride. Popular snacks include blueberry muffins, pies, and pastries, but the festival favorites are blueberry sundaes, made with creamy vanilla ice cream topped with a gooey blueberry sauce.

Hungarian Festival The people of New Brunswick honor their Hungarian ancestors at this June festival. In addition to tasting all manner of rich

Hungarian food, you can also enjoy Hungarian folk music and dancers and admire Hungarian art.

New Jersey Seafood Festival Each June seafood lovers descend on Belmar to devour lobster, clams, crabs, oysters, shrimp, and fish cooked every way imaginable. Besides all the food, there are also crab races, model boat competitions, music, and an arts-and-crafts fair.

Polka Spree by the Sea For four days each June, Wildwood kicks up its heels, as bands on the boardwalk provide the music for twelve hours of nonstop polka dancing each day.

Hambletonian Day America's premier harness race takes place in East Rutherford each August. Besides watching magnificent horses race around the track, kids can take pony rides and enjoy the performances of clowns, jugglers, and musicians.

Hambletonian Day

Festival of the Sea The highlight of this September event at Point Pleasant Beach is an inner-tube race in the ocean. Those who would rather stay on land can eat all types of seafood, listen to music, and watch a spectacular fireworks display.

Wings 'n Water Festival Stone Harbor celebrates southern New Jersey's coastal habitat with this September event that features environmental exhibits and workshops, displays by wildlife artists, salt-marsh safaris, and a seafood feast.

Scandinavian Fest People from throughout North America descend on Waterloo Village in Stanhope each September to perform the music of Norway, Iceland, Denmark, Finland, and Sweden. You can also stroll among crafts exhibits and attend music workshops.

Chatsworth Cranberry Festival Cranberries are everywhere at this October event in Chatsworth. Of course you can taste cranberry cakes, pies, relishes, jellies, pancakes, and honey. But there are also contests for the best cranberry-decorated hat and the most cranberry-colored car. Even the flower arrangements and the artwork must include cranberries. You can top off your cranberry-filled day by touring a cranberry bog.

Christmas Candlelight House Tours During December, you can travel back in time and get in the holiday spirit by touring two dozen of Cape May's quaint 19th-century homes and churches, all decked out in their holiday best.

Reenactment of Washington Crossing the Delaware Each December thousands of history buffs gather in Trenton to reenact George Washington and his troops crossing the Delaware River on Christmas night.

STATE STARS

William "Bud" Abbott (1895–1974), who was born in Asbury Park, was half of the wildly popular comedy team Abbott and Costello. In such fast-talking routines as "Who's on First?" the tall, thin Abbott played straight man to the chubby, excitable Lou Costello.

Abbott and Costello

Charles Addams (1912–1988) was a cartoonist who first became famous drawing morbid, spooky cartoons for the *New Yorker* magazine in the 1930s. He is best remembered for creating the comically ghoulish Addams Family. These characters were the basis of a television series in the 1960s and two popular movies in the 1990s. Addams was born in Westfield.

Edwin "Buzz" Aldrin (1930–   ), of Montclair, was an astronaut. In 1966, he became the third person to leave a spacecraft and "walk" in space. It was by far the longest and most successful spacewalk up to that time. Then, in 1969, Aldrin followed Neil Armstrong out of *Apollo 11* to become the second person to set foot on the moon.

Amiri Baraka (1934–   ) is an influential poet and playwright who usually writes about the plight of African Americans. In the 1960s, Baraka advocated black separatism. His 1964 award-winning play, *Dutchman*, was a landmark in African-American theater. In the 1970s, Baraka rejected black separatism when he became a passionate communist. Baraka was born Everett LeRoi Jones in Newark and changed his name when he converted to Islam.

Count Basie (1904–1984), a native of Red Bank, led one of the greatest jazz bands ever. As a child, Basie played drums before turning to the piano. He performed in other people's groups until he founded his own band in 1935, which became one of the leading bands of the swing era. Basie continued to lead his own orchestra into the 1980s.

Count Basie

Judy Blume (1938–   ), who was born in Elizabeth, writes frank books for young people. Her novels are renowned for their wit, honesty, and compassion. She first came to prominence in 1970 with her novel *Are You There God? It's Me, Margaret.* Her other well-known books include *Superfudge*, *Tales of a Fourth Grade Nothing*, and *Tiger Eyes*.

William Brennan (1906–1997) was a Supreme Court justice for 34 years. Brennan, who was born in Newark, was a justice on the New Jersey Supreme Court before being appointed to the U.S. Supreme Court in 1956. During his many years on the Court, he proved himself a solid defender of freedom of speech, religion, and other personal liberties.

Aaron Burr (1756–1836), of Newark, was a U.S. vice president who killed his longtime political rival Alexander Hamilton in a duel. This event ended Burr's political career. Later he was involved in a scheme to invade Spanish territory in the Southwest. He was tried for treason but acquitted.

Grover Cleveland (1837–1908) was the 22nd and the 24th president of the United States. He was the only native New Jerseyan to become president, the only president elected to two nonconsecutive terms, and the only president to get married in office. Cleveland was born in Caldwell.

Lou Costello (1906–1959) was half of the most popular comedy team of the 1940s. He and Bud Abbott were renowned for their fast-talking, carefully timed patter, such as their classic "Who's on First?" routine. They made many successful movies, including *In the Navy* and *Abbott and Costello Meet Frankenstein*. Costello was born in Paterson.

Stephen Crane (1871–1900) was a poet and novelist who is renowned for his brutally honest and pessimistic vision of life. Crane, who was born in Newark, began his career as a newspaper reporter covering the slums

of New York. His own poverty and the encounters he had as a journalist served as the basis of his first novel, *Maggie, a Girl of the Streets*. He is most famous for *The Red Badge of Courage*, a psychological study of a young Civil War soldier.

Stephen Crane

Thomas Edison (1847–1931), the world's most famous inventor, spent most of his adult life in New Jersey. Edison was born in Milan, Ohio, and became a telegraph operator in 1862. Two years later, he created his first invention, an automatic telegraph repeater. He eventually moved to the East Coast, and in 1876 he set up an invention factory in Menlo Park, New Jersey, hiring chemists, physicists, and mathematicians to help him solve problems. He later moved his research laboratory to West Orange. Edison's greatest accomplishments include perfecting the lightbulb and developing the phonograph and motion pictures.

Allen Ginsburg (1926–1997), a poet, was the leading spokesman for the "beat generation" of the 1950s, who railed against the constraints and conformity of the time. Ginsburg first gained prominence in 1956 for his poem "Howl," a long, angry cry of despair that denounced conventional society and social ills. Ginsberg's poetry is renowned for its vivid images and graphic language. He was born in Newark.

Whitney Houston (1963–   ), of Newark, is among the most popular contemporary singers. Her first album, *Whitney Houston*, hit number one on the pop charts in 1985, and the song "Saving All My Love for You," earned her a Grammy Award. When her second album, *Whitney*, was also a smash, she became the first popular singer to sell 10 million copies of each of her first two records. Houston is also a successful actress, having appeared in such hits as *The Bodyguard* and *Waiting to Exhale*.

Carl Lewis (1961–   ) is one of the greatest track and field athletes of all time and the winner of nine Olympic gold medals. In 1984, he became the second person in history to win four gold medals in a summer Olympics. He also won four straight gold medals in the long jump, from 1984 to 1996, becoming the second person to win the gold in the same event in four consecutive Olympics. Lewis was born in Birmingham, Alabama, and grew up in Willingsboro, New Jersey.

Jerry Lewis (1926–   ), a popular comedy actor of the 1950s and 1960s, was born in Newark. Early in his career, Lewis was part of a comedy team with Dean Martin. Beginning with *My Friend Irma* in 1949, the duo made 17 movies in which Lewis played hysterical, clumsy characters opposite Dean Martin's suave ladies' man. After the team broke up, Lewis directed and starred in his own films, such as *The Nutty Professor*. Today, he is perhaps best known for hosting the annual Jerry Lewis Telethon for Muscular Dystrophy, which has raised hundreds of millions of dollars to fight the disease.

Jerry Lewis

John McPhee (1931–   ), the author of more than 20 nonfiction books, is known for being able to make any subject interesting and for giving a balanced perspective on conflicting viewpoints. McPhee was born in Princeton and attended Princeton University. He had already written many books when he finally gained prominence in 1977 with the best-seller *Coming into the Country*, a book about Alaska. Although McPhee has written about subjects as varied as sports and travel, most of his writing has been about nature, including *The Pine Barrens*, about his native state.

Jack Nicholson (1937–   ), is a leading motion picture actor, famous for his menacing grin and nonconformist characters. Nicholson first drew attention in 1969 for his role as a lawyer who drops out of conventional society in *Easy Rider*. A string of great roles in such films as *Five Easy Pieces*, *Chinatown*, and *The Shining* made him famous. He has earned three Academy Awards, most recently for the 1997 film *As Good as It Gets*. Nicholson was born in Neptune.

Dorothy Parker (1893–1967) was a poet, short-story writer, and critic known for her dark, biting humor and elegant satire. Early in her career, Parker was a critic for the magazine *Vanity Fair*, but she was fired because she often wrote devastating pans of major plays. She then moved to the *New Yorker*, where she stayed until her first poetry collection, *Enough Rope*, was published and became a best-seller. In the 1920s and 1930s she was a member of the Algonquin Round Table, a group of writers who hung out at New York City's Algonquin Hotel and were famous for their witty conversation. Parker was born in West End.

Dorothy Parker

Paul Robeson

Paul Robeson (1898–1976) was a leading singer, famous
for his deep, rich voice. Robeson was born in Princeton
and attended Rutgers University, where he became the
first black all-American football player and won first
prize in the college's speaking competition four years
in a row. After graduating from Columbia University
Law School, he joined a New York law firm, but his
career was cut short because of racism. He then turned
to performing, appearing in such works as *Othello* and *Show Boat* and
becoming one of the first African Americans to play serious roles. Robeson
was also politically active, fighting for black rights around the world. His
friendship with the Soviet Union eventually brought criticism from the U.S.
government, and his career declined sharply in the early 1950s.

Ruth St. Denis (1879–1968), one of the founders of modern dance in the
United States, was born Ruth Dennis in Newark. At the time, the only
types of dance performed in the United States were ballet and vaudeville.
In 1906, St. Denis appeared in her own work, *Radha*, which was based
upon dances of India. Throughout her career, she showed many Asian
influences and stressed individuality and expressive movements. In
1915, she cofounded an influential school of dance. For many years
it was the training ground of every important American dancer and
choreographer.

Antonin Scalia (1936–   ), a Supreme Court justice, was born in Trenton. Scalia was a law professor and an official in the U.S. Justice
Department before being appointed to the U.S. Court of Appeals in
1982. Since being named to the Supreme Court in 1986, he has become
known for his sharp intellect and his strict conservatism.

Norman Schwartzkopf

Norman Schwartzkopf (1934–   ) is a retired U.S. Army general who planned and executed the United States–led attack on Iraq during the Persian Gulf War. Schwartzkopf, whose father was a general in World War I, attended the U.S. Military Academy at West Point, served in Vietnam, and then rose through the ranks to become a general. He was born in Trenton.

Frank Sinatra (1915–1998) was one of the most popular singers in U.S. history. Sinatra, who was born in Hoboken, began singing in clubs as a teenager. With his relaxed, resonant style, he became the best-known singer of the big band era. He was also the first performer whom girls screamed and swooned over. He was a darker, more melancholy figure in the 1950s, singing songs of loneliness and last chances. Sinatra also acted in movies, earning an Academy Award for playing a feisty soldier in *From Here to Eternity*. Sinatra continued performing into his eighties.

Bruce Springsteen (1949–   ) is a popular rock-and-roll performer who grew up in Freehold and began his career in Asbury Park. Beginning in the 1970s, he became the voice of working-class New Jersey, singing songs about dead-end jobs and young people searching for freedom. Springsteen became a superstar in 1984, when his album *Born in the U.S.A.* sold 20 million copies and stayed in the top ten on the charts for two years.

Alfred Stieglitz (1864–1946) was a photographer and gallery director who led the movement to have photography recognized as an art. Stieglitz began entering his photographs in competitions in the 1880s, winning over 150 exhibitions. Although at first he photographed picturesque scenes, his images later became more abstract, using lines and shapes to convey emotion. His 291 gallery in New York became the leading promoter of modern art in the United States, showing works by such modernists as Pablo Picasso. Stieglitz was born in Hoboken.

Meryl Streep (1949–   ) is one of the country's best film actresses, renowned for her ability to disappear into any role. She was a well-respected stage actress before she made her screen debut in 1977 in *Julia*. Throughout her career, she has given one stunning performance after another in such films as *Sophie's Choice* and *Silkwood*, racking up ten Academy Award nominations and two wins. Streep was born in Summit.

John Travolta (1954–   ) is a popular movie actor, known for his good-humored charisma. In the 1970s, Travolta became a teen idol for his role as a dim-witted high school student in the television comedy *Welcome Back, Kotter*. He soon appeared in a string of hit films, including *Grease* and *Saturday Night Fever*. In the 1980s, he had few good roles, and he fell into obscurity. But his career was rejuvenated in 1994 when he earned an Oscar nomination for his role as an amiable hit man in *Pulp Fiction*, and he is again one of the country's leading actors.

John Travolta

Sarah Vaughan (1924–1990), who was born in Newark, was one of the world's best jazz vocalists. Her career took off after she won the Apollo Theater's amateur night contest in Harlem in 1942 and was invited to join Earl Hines's band. During her long career, she was praised for her rich voice, amazing range, and improvisational ability,

Selman Waksman (1888–1973) was a scientist who discovered several medicines, called antibiotics, that saved countless lives. Waksman was born in the Ukraine and moved to the United States in 1910 to attend Rutgers University in New Brunswick. He eventually became a professor at Rutgers, where he did research on antibiotics. His discoveries enabled doctors to cure such diseases as tuberculosis. Waksman was awarded the Nobel Prize in medicine in 1952.

Selman Waksman

Christine Todd Whitman (1946–   ) is the first female governor of New Jersey. Whitman was born in New York but grew up in Oldwick, New Jersey, where her parents were prominent members of the Republican Party. After narrowly losing a race for the U.S. Senate in 1990, Whitman was elected governor in 1993 and reelected in 1997.

William Carlos Williams (1883–1963) was a poet who had both an interest in everyday language and subjects and a romantic impulse. Williams grew up in Rutherford and returned there after he earned a medical degree. He spent 40 years working as a doctor, writing poetry during his spare time. His most famous work is a long poem called *Paterson*.

TOUR THE STATE

Waterloo Village (Stanhope) Step into the past at the village, which has 23 restored homes and buildings filled with period furnishings. As you wander through the village, costumed guides explain what you're seeing, and craftspeople work in the blacksmith shop and sawmill.

Franklin Mineral Museum (Franklin) This museum houses the world's largest collection of fluorescent minerals, which were found nearby. It also includes a replica of a zinc mine just like the one where miners found the amazing rocks.

Great Falls Historic Landmark District (Paterson) Smack in the middle of Paterson, you can visit the 77-foot-high Great Falls of the Passaic, along with some of the mills that the falls powered.

Liberty Science Center (Jersey City) Two highlights of this hands-on science museum are the one hundred-foot-long Touch Tunnel, where you have to find your way through the pitch black using your sense of touch, and the Illusion Labyrinth, which is filled with optical illusions.

Newark Museum (Newark) A planetarium, a sculpture garden, and an important collection of Native American art are all part of this wide-ranging museum.

Sandy Hook Lighthouse (Highlands) The oldest operating lighthouse in the United States, the Sandy Hook Lighthouse has been warning ships of the shore since 1764.

Edison National Historic Site (West Orange) While visiting Edison's laboratory, you'll see demonstrations of early phonographs and watch *The Great Train Robbery*, an early motion picture filmed with Edison's equipment.

New Jersey State Aquarium (Camden) At this vast aquarium, you can touch a shark, admire a coral reef, and put on a helmet that lets you listen to dolphins communicating with one another.

Lucy, the Margate Elephant (Margate City) Climb the stairs inside this six-story-high elephant for a nice view from her back. Lucy was built in 1881.

Barnegat Bay Decoy and Baymen's Museum (Tuckerton) This museum celebrates the sea culture that once thrived on Barnegat Bay. You can learn all about boatbuilding, clamming, and oystering, as well as admire many beautiful hand-carved wildfowl decoys.

Black River & Western Railroad (Flemington) You can take an 11-mile ride on a vintage steam-powered train through the farmland of western New Jersey.

Delaware and Raritan Canal State Park (Stockton) This 60-mile-long park along an old canal is the perfect place to hike, bike, ride horses, and fish. It also contains 17 historic buildings to explore.

Morristown National Historic Park (Morristown) This park preserves the area where the Continental army spent the brutal winter of 1779–1780. The site includes a museum housing 18th-century weapons and George Washington memorabilia. You can also visit the mansion where Washington spent the winter and replicas of log huts where the soldiers lived.

Six Flags Wild Safari Animal Park (Jackson) More than 1,200 animals including zebras, bisons, and giraffes live at this wildlife preserve. As you drive through the park, animals may come right up to your window.

Batsto Village (Batsto) This preserved village re-creates life in the Pine Barrens of the 19th century. At the site, you'll learn about the early ironmaking industry and about what life was like for the people who worked there.

Wharton State Forest (Hammonton) This forest is an ideal place for outdoors enthusiasts to hike, camp, fish, and especially canoe in the mysterious Pine Barrens.

Edwin B. Forsythe National Wildlife Refuge (Oceanville) A huge variety of birds spend part of the year at this refuge, including peregrine falcons, piping plovers, and snowy egrets.

Historic Cold Spring Village (Cape May) You can see craftspeople demonstrating such skills as spinning and weaving at this re-creation of a 19th-century village. You can also visit an old railroad depot, school, and jail.

Historic Cold Spring Village

Cape May Point State Park (Cape May) Bird-watchers flock to this park to glimpse hawks and other migrating birds. Sometimes you can also see dolphins from the beach.

Wetlands Institute (Stone Harbor) The institute is filled with displays and hands-on exhibits about the wetlands of southern New Jersey. You can also climb a tower that provides a fabulous view of the surrounding area and walk a trail that leads out into a salt marsh.

FUN FACTS

New Jersey boasts a few firsts when it comes to sports. The first professional basketball game was played in Trenton in 1896. The first college football game was played in New Brunswick in 1869. Princeton played Rutgers, and Rutgers won.

The world's first drive-in movie theater opened June 6, 1933, outside of Camden. It had room for 500 cars.

The first dinosaur skeleton unearthed in North America was found by a farmer in Haddonfield, New Jersey, in 1858. He didn't realize he had found something so unusual until he mentioned his discovery to a scientist 20 years later.

FIND OUT MORE

To find out more about New Jersey, look for these titles in your local library or bookstore.

BOOKS

General State Books

Fradin, Dennis Brindell. *New Jersey*. Chicago: Children's Press, 1993.

Fredeen, Charles. *New Jersey*. Minneapolis, MN: Lerner, 1993.

Lewis, Paul. *The Beauty of New Jersey*. Portland, OR: LTA/Renaissance, 1991.

Topper, Frank, and Charles A. Wills. *A Historical Album of New Jersey*. Brookfield, CT: Millbrook Press, 1995.

Special Interest Books

Giblin, James. *Charles A. Lindbergh: A Human Hero*. New York: Clarion Books, 1997.

Gleiter, Jan, and Kathleen Thompson. *Molly Pitcher*. Milwaukee, WI: Raintree, 1987.

Grumet, Robert S. *The Lenapes*. New York: Chelsea House, 1989.

Lafferty, Peter. *Albert Einstein*. New York: Bookwright Press, 1992.

Lampton, Christopher. *Thomas Alva Edison*. New York: Franklin Watts, 1988.

McCloy, James F., and Ray Miller Jr. *The Jersey Devil*. Wallingford, PA: Middle Atlantic Press, 1976.

Tanaka, Shelley. *The Disaster of the Hindenburg: The Last Flight of the Greatest Airship Ever Built*. New York: Scholastic/Madison Press, 1993.

Wade, Mary Dodson. *Amelia Earhart: Flying for Adventure*. Brookfield, CT: Millbrook Press, 1994.

VIDEOTAPES

Portrait of America: New Jersey. New York: Turner Program Services, Inc., Ambrose Video Publishing, Inc., 1984.

INTERNET

http://www.state.nj.us
  This is the official New Jersey state website.

http://www.state.nj.us/pinelands/
  Go to this site for information about the Pinelands.

INDEX

Page numbers for charts, graphs, and illustrations are in boldface.